MW01298060

'THIS IS WHAT THE TOP FEELS LIKE'

Brian Kelly and the greatest team in Cincinnati football history

Cover design and layout by Heather Koch

Photos courtesy of the University of Cincinnati Athletic Dept. except where noted

ISBN: 9781686630026

Dedication

To all the players and coaches at the University of Cincinnati who fought the good fight down through the years to make Cincinnati football the outstanding program it is today.

Acknowledgements

When I was first assigned to cover University of Cincinnati basketball while working at the now-defunct Cincinnati Post in 1986, I volunteered to cover the football team too, not because I was into football that much, and not because it was considered a major beat at the time, but because I thought Cincinnati football was a fascinating story.

Here was a football program that had labored in the shadow of the basketball program for years. The program had no conference affiliation, a crumbling stadium, and sub-par facilities compared with other Division I schools. But the administration had always resisted calls from the faculty to disband the program to save the school money.

The Cincinnati football team absorbed its share of beatings while I was covering it, more than its share really, especially during those early years under Dave Currey. But I always admired the players who continued to soldier on against tremendous odds. I never imagined that one day the Bearcats would become a Top 10 national program with back-to-back appearances in the Orange Bowl and the Sugar Bowl, narrowly missing a chance to play for the national championship in 2009.

This book is a tribute to the players and coaches from the 2009 team, the only team in school history to produce an unbeaten regular season. It's also a tribute to those who came before them, coaches such as Currey, Tim Murphy, Rick Minter, Mark Dantonio and all their assistant coaches.

Thanks to Brian Kelly for cooperating with this venture, who to the players who put together the best season in Cincinnati football history for their willingness to share their memories and personal stories with me. Special thanks to Ben Guidugli, who helped me to get in touch with many of the players I interviewed for the book.

Also thanks to Ryan Koslen, Cincinnati's associate athletic director/communications who has been the primary media contact for the football program since 2008. Ryan has helped me over the years more times than I can count; to Cincinnati athletic director Mike Bohn, who hired me to write for the school's website when I left the Cincinnati Enquirer in 2014, and who has always supported me in the book projects I've undertaken since; and to Mo Egger, the WCKY-AM radio personality, who proofread the book for me.

Also thanks to my good friend Jack Brennan, a former Cincinnati Bengals public relations director, and before that a standout beat reporter in his own right, who edited this book with his usual insight and good humor; to my daughter, Heather, whom I corrupted in her formative years with my twisted sense of humor and love of sports. She worked her usual designing magic with this book while displaying remarkable patience with my many computer shortcomings. And, as always, to Rose, my wife of 40 years who has stuck with me through life's ups and downs, which have now included the writing and publishing of eight books. Her gentle touch in making suggestions without judgment, and her unfailing support for everything I do means more to me than she will ever know.

Contents

1

'Clearly the Best Team I've Ever Seen'

There's no greater authority on Cincinnati Bearcats football than Jim Kelly Jr. The former Cincinnati receiver started doing color commentary on radio broadcasts of Cincinnati games in 1988, Dave Currey's final year as head coach. He did two years under Currey's successor, Tim Murphy, then stepped away for a year. He came back in 1994 and has been doing the games ever since.

As a player, Kelly led the Bearcats in receiving for three straight years (1973-74-75), and in 2017 he was inducted into the school's James P. Kelly Athletics Hall of Fame, which is named for his father, Jim Kelly Sr. The elder Kelly played for the Bearcats from 1947 to 1950, and was a two-time all-Mid-American Conference selection, followed by a long career as a coach and administrator at the school before he retired in 1994.

Cincinnati football has been a major part of Kelly Jr.'s life for as long as he can remember. He's seen the program up-close at its lowest and at its highest, so you can trust his assessment of Brian Kelly's 2009 Bearcats, who went 12-0 during the regular season before losing to Florida in the Sugar Bowl.

"Clearly it was the best team I've ever seen," Kelly said. "There are probably some folks from the '50s who would argue with that, but I don't know how you can. It was a magical year. To have it get to the level that we're talking about in 2009, to see an undefeated team, I never thought I'd see that. I never thought I'd see a New Year's Day bowl game."

Some of the players from the 2009 team believe that their accomplishments were never celebrated properly because their banquet was overshadowed by Brian Kelly's departure. Forced to play Florida in the Sugar Bowl without the architect of their offense and their master motivator, they were unceremoniously thumped.

This is the story of that magical season and its painful conclusion. It's the story of how a collection of blue-collar players came together in an unlikely place, and inspired by a cutting-edge coach whose greatest accomplishments to that point had been in Division II, rose to take their place, however briefly, among the bluebloods of college football. And it's the story of Kelly's departure, why his stay at Cincinnati ended the way it did, why the players reacted with such fury when he left, and how they feel about their former coach today.

No other Cincinnati football team produced an undefeated regular season unless you count 1886 and 1887, when the Bearcats went 2-0 and 1-0 playing against Mt. Auburn and Woodward High School. No other Cincinnati team came within one second of playing for the national championship. And no other Cincinnati team played in the Sugar Bowl a year after playing in the Orange Bowl.

"You had a different pop in your step going to work every day," said Mike Thomas, the Cincinnati athletic director from 2005 to 2011. "People came to work with a Kool-Aid smile. We had a couple of years of that and tremendous momentum. There was a lot of electricity."

Thomas hired Brian Kelly (no relation to Jim) to replace Mark Dantonio in December 2006, after Dantonio left to become the head coach at Michigan State. It turned out to be one of the best hires in the history of Cincinnati athletics.

At the time, the Bearcats had just finished their second season in the Big East Conference after nine years in Conference USA, having finally landed in a conference that provided them with a path to the national championship. They took the first steps in the new league under Dantonio, then made a giant leap under Kelly, who went 34-6 during his three years at Cincinnati. The fans responded in a big way.

"Mark had some good years, and we had some pretty good players and we had some success," Thomas said. "But when I first showed up there the stadium was half full. It wasn't like my staff and I were some marketing geniuses. Because of winning, Nippert Stadium was pretty much at capacity every Saturday."

Bearcats football had long been an afterthought in the Cincinnati sports lineup behind Major League Baseball's Reds, the National Football League's Bengals, and Cincinnati and Xavier basketball. But during 2008 and 2009, especially 2009 when the Bearcats repeated as Big East Conference champions, it suddenly became cool to be a Cincinnati football fan, maybe for the first time ever.

This is What the Top Feels Like

The crowds were so big the school had to implement a new student ticket policy. Cincinnati had routinely set aside 6,000 seats for students at its home games, but for one game 10,000 showed up. Students began camping out for tickets.

"We were superstars at Cincinnati," said defensive end

The Cincinnati student section shares a winning moment with defensive back Brad Jones after the Bearcats knock off West Virginia at Nippert Stadium.

Alex Daniels. "When you walked around everybody knew who you were. It was like being the Beatles in college. It was the best time of my life. We changed the demographic of the program."

Before he took the Cincinnati job, Brian Kelly had heard all the stories about Cincinnati's lack of an appetite for college football. The Queen City was a baseball town, an NFL town, a college basketball town, and a high school sports town, but certainly not a college football town.

Kelly made it his mission to prove that theory wrong.

"I've always felt like Cincinnati had no appetite for losing football, and that proved to be true," he said. "Like most cities, they're going to support what is successful. Well-played sports, whether it's soccer or basketball, if it's done right, they'll support it.

So it was a validation in my eyes when they came out and they were sitting in the trees for games. That's what the city is all about. They're going to back you if you do it the right way."

In late 2009, the program's future was bright under Kelly, who had signed a contract extension through the 2013 season on June 22. When he requested new practice fields complete with a bubble to allow his team to practice indoors during inclement weather, the Cincinnati administration acceded to his wishes. Fundraising for the facility was well underway.

The 2009 team still owns school records for wins (12), road wins (6), points (502), touchdowns (66), touchdown passes (39), kickoff return yards (1,540), fewest fumbles (11), fewest fumbles lost (2), and fewest turnovers (10).

To grasp what that level of success meant for the Cincinnati football program, consider that the Bearcats didn't play in a single bowl game for 47 years, from the end of the 1950 season until 1997, when they defeated Utah State in the inaugural Humanitarian Bowl in Boise, Idaho. To secure the invitation to a bowl game -- even one that few fans had heard of -- then-athletic director Bob Goin had to promise bowl officials that the Bearcats' historically accomplished basketball program would play at Boise State the following season.

The Humanitarian Bowl was followed by a series appearances in minor bowls until 2008, Kelly's second year as head coach, when the Bearcats won the Big East title and earned the right to play in the Orange Bowl, where they lost to Virginia Tech in Miami Gardens, Florida.

While the Bearcats were reaching heights that many long-time followers believed they could never achieve, things weren't going so well 350 miles northwest of Cincinnati in South Bend, Indiana, where Charlie Weis' five-year stay at Notre Dame appeared to be coming to an end. Under Weis, the Fighting Irish had started the season with a 6-2 record only to finish with four straight losses. With every loss, the outcry for Weis to be fired grew louder.

Because of the success he was having at Cincinnati, and how he was doing it, Kelly's name kept popping up in the media on lists of potential candidates to replace Weis. Cincinnati fans, the Bearcat players, and most of all Thomas, were following the developments in South Bend closely, knowing that when Weis was fired Notre Dame athletic director Jack Swarbrick would have an interest in Kelly despite the contract extension he had recently signed.

Even with the rumors swirling, the Cincinnati players focused on the task at hand, which was to finish off their perfect season. They staged a miraculous comeback to beat Pittsburgh in their final regular season game, which clinched their second straight Big East championship, and they missed qualifying for the BCS national championship game only because the officials in the Big 12 championship game between Texas and Nebraska decided to put one second back on the clock at the end of the game, enough to allow the Longhorns to kick the game-winning field goal.

Five days after their emotional victory over Pitt, with all signs pointing to Kelly's departure, the news leaked out on the day of the Cincinnati football banquet that Kelly had indeed accepted the

Wide receiver Armon Binns celebrates with his teammates after his catch that tied the game in the Bearcats' win over Pitt.

Notre Dame job. When that happened, the air came out of Cincinnati's football balloon. Joy was replaced by anger and the program was sent reeling. Three weeks later the Bearcats were blown out by Florida in the Sugar Bowl.

The greatest season in Cincinnati football history didn't end well, but it remains one of the best stories in the history of Queen City sports.

"It was really the best three years in Cincinnati football," said Jason Kelce, an offensive lineman on the 2009 team who went on to become a star in the NFL. "I don't think it's close."

The 2009 Bearcats outscored their opponents, 502-300, an average of 38.6 points to 23.1. They gained 5,817 yards of total offense to 4,862 for their opponents. They ranked fourth nationally in scoring offense, eighth in passing offense (308.8 yards per game), and 11th in total offense (5,817 yards). They were second in kickoff returns (28.5-yard average) and tied for eighth in sacks (37.0). They were 13th in turnover margin (plus nine), fourth in tackles for loss (110), and fourth in fourth down conversions (69.23 percent).

Perhaps wide receiver Armon Binns summed up that season best: "It was like, this is what the top feels like."

2

'There Goes Mardy'

No one saw this coming. After winning 11 games that lifted them to a No. 5 national ranking with one of the most powerful offenses in college football, the Cincinnati Bearcats were on the verge of getting blown out by No. 14 Pittsburgh in the game that would determine the Big East champion. They trailed, 31-10, with 1:26 remaining in the first half.

Despite the importance of the game, the talk among Cincinnati fans during the week leading up to it was more about Kelly and his possible departure for Notre Dame than it was about the game itself. Many of the fans who showed up for Kelly's weekly radio show that week carried red towels with black lettering that read, "CINCY COMMITTED TO KELLY."

When the teams took the field for the 12:07 p.m. kickoff, the temperature was 30 degrees with snowflakes whipping around Heinz Field, where 63,387 fans were eager to see their Panthers ruin the Bearcats' perfect season.

Pitt was 8-3 overall, 5-1 in the Big East. Cincinnati was 11-0, 6-0. A Pitt victory would leave the Panthers and the Bearcats tied for first place, but Pitt, by winning its head-to-head matchup with Cincinnati, would earn the automatic bid to the Sugar Bowl in New

9

This is What the Top Feels Like

Orleans, relegating Cincinnati to a likely slot in the Meineke Car Care Bowl in Charlotte, North Carolina. After playing in the Orange Bowl the previous season and steamrolling through their first 11 opponents, that wasn't at all what the Bearcats had in mind.

Cincinnati quarterback Tony Pike, who earlier in the season had been considered a legitimate Heisman Trophy candidate, was struggling through a horrendous day. He completed only eight of 23 passes for 84 yards in the first half with no touchdowns and two interceptions. Pitt was dominating the Cincinnati defense behind the running of 5-foot-9, 196-pound freshman running back Dion Lewis, who gained 108 yards with one touchdown in the first half alone.

"We knew going in that this was for the Big East championship," Pike said, "but it was also for a BCS bowl game and the possibility of playing for the national championship.

A crowd of 63,387 showed up at Heinz Field in Pittsburgh eager to see the Panthers end the Bearcats' perfect season.

But if we lose to Pittsburgh, we're not talking about that season anymore. What I remember the most about the week leading up to the game is that it was probably the most locked-in week we had that season of guys understanding what was at stake and what we were going into at Pittsburgh, the crowd we were going to be facing, and the weather forecast of wind and snow. We knew it was going to be a tough atmosphere."

Cincinnati had been effectively shut out of the BCS games as a member of Conference USA, with no realistic hope of ever competing for a national championship. But in 2005, when the Bearcats joined the Big East -- one of six conferences designated as major, or BCS conferences -- they were guaranteed an automatic bid to a major bowl if they could win the Big East title, as they did in 2008.

And now, at what appeared to be the high point in the 123-year history of Cincinnati football, they were being pummeled on national television as they attempted to complete the first undefeated regular season in the program's history. During the first half, it appeared as if Pike was overwhelmed by the enormity of the moment.

"Whether he was pressing or whether he didn't want to be the guy to mess it up, Tony wasn't really cutting it loose like he normally does," Binns said. "Tony had a gunslinger mentality, and that's what made him so special. He was trying so hard not to do the wrong thing that it was putting him in bad situations."

Many of the players on that team now say their confidence never wavered despite their poor first-half performance. They claim they knew they would come back to win no matter how far behind they were. But not everyone was so confident during that sobering first half.

"When we were down a lot of people were thinking, 'We're going to lose,'" said defensive back Aaron Webster. "The snow is coming down like crazy. We're not throwing good. We can't get our offense going, and we can't really stop them. Everything was coming to a head at once."

Pittsburgh coach Dave Wannstedt's game plan was working perfectly because of the success the diminutive but powerful Lewis was having slicing through the Cincinnati defense.

"The biggest thing I was concerned with was somebody busting something and giving them an easy score," Wannstedt said. "So our plan going in was to run the ball and play a little keep-away, which we did. We thought we could run it. We didn't think we could run it that good."

It's not like the Cincinnati defense hadn't been warned about Lewis, who rushed for 1,799 yards that season, which ranked third nationally, and was named the Big East Offensive Player of the Year.

"All we kept hearing about coming into the game was Dion Lewis, Dion Lewis, Dion Lewis," Webster said. "So I'm like, this guy is a buck-eighty, five-eight or five-nine on a good day. He can't be that much. I'm looking at tape and I'm thinking I'm going to get this guy in space and I'm going to go for a kill shot every time I get a shot at him. I figure there's only so much a person of that stature can take. But he was shifty. And trying to tackle a guy like that when it's snowing like that and with the ice, you're pretty much on a skating

Aaron Webster and the rest of the Bearcats found out how tough it was to bring down Pitt's Dion Lewis.

rink. And you've got a guy who loves to do jump cuts, shifts. Tackling a guy like that is not easy."

Pitt took an early lead on Lewis' four-yard run. Cincinnati answered on its next possession with a seven-play, 66-yard drive that ended with Jacob Ramsey's two-yard touchdown run to tie the score at 7-7 at the end of the first quarter. Wide receiver Jonathan Baldwin scored on a 22-yard pass from quarterback Bill Stull early in the second quarter. Cincinnati's Jake Rogers kicked a 20-yard field goal to make it 14-10.

The Panthers then scored 17 unanswered points on a 40-yard touchdown pass from Stull to Baldwin; a 33-yard field goal by Dan Hutchins; and a three-yard touchdown run by Stull that gave them their 21-point lead. The Bearcats' worst nightmare was coming true.

"I remember at times sitting on that bench and that crowd was roaring," Pike said. "The stadium was actually shaking. Everyone's singing 'Sweet Caroline' and you're down 31-10 and nothing's going right.

"When a team is running the ball the way Pittsburgh was, you start counting possessions," Pike continued. "You start to think, 'OK, we're down 14, we're down 21, we've got to make something happen.' You try to force a throw in or try to make something happen that's not there. You start trying to chase possessions instead of staying inside your offense. That's where it got away from us in the first half."

After Stull's touchdown, tight end Ben Guidugli spotted teammates Binns and wide receiver D.J. Woods sitting on the bench with tears in their eyes. He knelt on one knee in front of them and gave them a tongue-lashing.

"I told them to knock that shit off," Guidugli said. "We've got two quarters of football to go. Then I turn around and there goes Mardy, and everybody was going crazy."

The Panthers had kicked off to Mardy Gilyard, the best kick returner in the league, possibly the entire country. As Pike put it, "Pittsburgh gave us the gift of kicking to Mardy."

No other player on the Cincinnati roster had the ability to change a game the way Gilyard could. The previous year at Hawaii he had helped the Bearcats overcome a 14-point deficit, scoring the winning touchdown on a 69-yard pass from quarterback Dustin Grutza with 4:42 to play. Now his teammates and his coaches were looking to Gilyard, almost pleading with him, to make another play.

The coaching staff told Gilyard before the game not to run the ball out of the end zone on a kickoff return. But with the Bearcats in such a deep hole and the season on the line, that plan was thrown out. Associate head coach Kerry Coombs approached Gilyard before the kick and said, "I don't care where it is, you take it back. We've got to have a play. We've got to have something happen. He said, 'I got you, boss.'"

Ben Guidugli tries to raise the spirits of his teammates, D.J. Woods, 3, and Armon Bins during the first half of the Pittsburgh game.
Photo by: Ron Padretto

Gilyard caught the ball at the one-yard line and began to make his way down the field. He feinted one way then the other to avoid would-be tacklers. When he reached the Cincinnati 30, he cut inside and was sprung at the 33 by a block from Demetrius Jones, a once-heralded quarterback who had transferred to Cincinnati two years earlier from Notre Dame. Jones had undergone clavicle surgery, and had been moved to linebacker for his senior year. Now he was on special teams, sprinting down the field to clear a path for Gilyard, performing a role he never could have envisioned when he was a Parade Magazine prep All-American quarterback in Chicago.

After Jones' block, Gilyard cut sharply to his left and headed toward the sideline where he outran the coverage and burst into the end zone to complete a 99-yard return. His teammates jumped up and down on the sideline and cheered wildly.

"When I got it, I saw a crease and stuck my head out and I saw Demetrius Jones, who comes out of nowhere and just 'smack,'" Gilyard said. "When I saw him do that, I cut off him, and there was a crease there and I followed the crease. When I got to the 50, I knew I was going to score. There were two guys who had a nice angle on me, but I made them run the width of the field and they eventually ran out of gas. That gave us the boost of energy that we needed."

To Binns, it was only logical that Gilyard would be the player to shake the Bearcats out of their doldrums. The fact that he did it in such dramatic fashion only made the impact greater.

"It just felt like finally, finally we caught that break," Binns said. "We were chipping away, we were battling, and finally we caught that break."

The Bearcats got the ball back at the Pitt 35 with 51 seconds remaining before halftime, but Elijah Fields intercepted a Pike pass at the Pitt 30-yard line and returned it to the Cincinnati 44. Cincinnati's Webster then intercepted Stull's pass at the Cincinnati

23 and returned it 31 yards to the Pitt 46. On the last play of the half, the Bearcats' Rogers attempted a 55-yard field goal that fell short.

As the players walked off the field toward the locker rooms, Cincinnati trailed, 31-17, and had gained only 147 yards to Pitt's 232. Kelly turned to Pike and said, perhaps out of frustration, perhaps as motivation for the second half, "You're going to apologize for ruining this team's perfect season."

3

An Unconventional Coach

Brian Kelly was introduced as the 37th head football coach in Cincinnati history at the Kingsgate Marriott Conference Center on the Cincinnati campus on December 4, 2006. He was 45 and had spent the last three years at Central Michigan, where he led the Chippewas to a 19-16 record, with a Mid-American Conference championship in 2006. Before Kelly's arrival in 2004, Central Michigan had won a total of 12 games in the previous four seasons and had suffered through seven straight losing seasons. Previously, Kelly was the head coach at Division II Grand Valley State in Allendale, Michigan, for 13 seasons. He led the Lakers to national championships in 2003 and 2004 and developed a reputation as an offensive innovator.

At Cincinnati, he took over a program that had been cast in the mold of Dantonio, who had been hired in 2003 as the head coach by Goin. He replaced Rick Minter and was charged with taking Cincinnati into the Big East. Dantonio built his program around defense, physical toughness and a conservative, run-oriented offense.

Kelly understood the value of toughness, too, but from the outset of his time at Cincinnati he was focused mostly on offense.

This is What the Top Feels Like

On the day he was hired, he promised a wide open passing attack, much to the delight of Cincinnati fans. But that was only part of what he said he would deliver.

Cincinnati fans where excited when Brian Kelly promised a wide-open passing attack at his introductory press conference.

"Not only will you see a football game, which is obviously important," he said. "You're going to see an event. We will unify the University of Cincinnati to get an atmosphere that is electric. We want to throw the ball around a little bit."

Cincinnati had never seen a football coach like Kelly. He was supremely confident, determined to succeed at a high level, and not afraid to hurt feelings. He wasn't shy about making demands, not just on his players and coaching staff, but also on the administration. He knew where he wanted to take the program, and what it would take to get it there. No one was going to stand in his way. Occasionally he rubbed people the wrong way, but that was of no concern to him. He was there to change the course of the program.

At the time, attracting fans to Nippert Stadium was so difficult that the Cincinnati athletic department instituted a plan that required fans who wanted to purchase season basketball tickets to also buy season football tickets. As Goin once said, "I tried everything to get fans into that stadium except parachuting them in."

As Kelly contemplated the next step in his coaching career after Central Michigan, he envisioned something in Cincinnati that few others did: a program with the potential to compete for a national championship.

"More than anything else," Kelly said, "it was the idea of a program in the heartland that had Midwest roots, Ohio roots, and in many ways I looked at it as a program that had what I felt was untapped potential. I thought that Cincinnati had been perceived by many to be fundamentally a basketball school. It left me the opportunity to build something that had not been built before."

From a pure football standpoint, Kelly found the program in better shape than he had expected, thanks to the work Dantonio and his staff had done before him. In addition, the construction of Varsity Village, a major upgrade of the athletics facilities engineered by Goin, moved the Bearcats closer to what the major programs had. The locker rooms, meeting rooms, weight room and training room had all been significantly improved,

The Bearcats played their home games in a charming, throwback stadium located in the center of campus that Kelly later called "the Wrigley Field of college football." Cincinnati first played on the site in 1902. The actual brick-and-concrete structure was dedicated on November 8, 1924. During Kelly's time at Cincinnati, Nippert Stadium's official seating capacity was 35,097.

"Mark Dantonio had developed and instilled some principles that are absolutely crucial to turning a program around -- toughness and in particular playing hard," Kelly said. "It was a team that had a hardness to them. It was the periphery that needed a lot of work."

Kelly knew that in order to attract fans, Cincinnati needed to do more than require basketball fans to buy football tickets. He would have to venture into the community and sell the program himself. He met with any group that would allow him to sell his vision for the program, showing up to talk to youth football teams, larger organized groups, even small gatherings in bars.

"It needed me to be at Chicken on the Run," Kelly said, referring to a café in suburban Deer Park. "It needed that kind of support. That really was the big transition."

He also understood that the best way to attract fans was not only to win, but to do so in an entertaining fashion. One of his first moves was to bring in Ben Mauk, a transfer from Wake Forest, to play quarterback in 2007. Mauk passed for 3,121 yards and a school-record 31 touchdowns while leading the Bearcats to a 10-3 record, 4-3 in the Big East. That was good enough for third place and an invitation to the PapaJohn's.com Bowl in Birmingham, Alabama, where Cincinnati defeated Southern Mississippi 31-21. But Kelly had much higher goals than the PapaJohn's.com Bowl.

Kelly's offensive acumen wasn't the only attribute that distinguished him from other recent Cincinnati coaches. His entire approach to running a program was different from anything the school had seen before.

Dantonio had maintained a close relationship with most, if not all of his players. At times he would even knock on Gilyard's door early in the morning to make sure he got to class on time. "He always reminded me, 'I told your mama I was going to make a man out of you,'" Gilyard said. "Coach D kind of spoiled us. He cared about us as people. He knew my mom and my grandma. BK was totally opposite."

Players couldn't walk into Kelly's office for an impromptu chat as they could with Dantonio. They had to make an appointment. When Butch Jones was hired to replace Kelly, he made a point of letting the media know that one of the first things he did when he met with his players was to write his cell phone number on the board in the team meeting room so they would always have access to him.

If Kelly's players needed someone to talk to, they went to their position coach, to trainer Bob Mangine, or to strength coach Paul Longo. In essence, they said, Kelly was more like a CEO running a business.

"Mark Dantonio was very hands-on with the players and wanted to know everything about you," Pike said. "He implemented Bible study, things like that. Brian Kelly was a football coach. That's all he wanted to be and that's all he was at UC. There wasn't a time when his office door was always open. "

The players say Kelly more closely resembled an NFL coach than a rah-rah college coach.

"He was very organized," Kelce said. "He had a very businesslike approach. Do your job. Do what you're told. Dantonio was very much a father figure to a lot of guys on the team. He was a very religious man, a very family-oriented person. He made all of that known. He involved everybody's parents. That's just kind of who he was."

There was also a major difference in the way the two coaches conducted practice. Dantonio was a perfectionist who would start practice over if he didn't like what he was seeing. Kelly liked to run his practices at a fast pace. His goal was to finish in an hour and a half, although that's not to say he wouldn't make his players redo a drill now and again if he didn't like the way they executed it.

He wanted minimal coaching on the field during practice when the Bearcats were doing their actual game preparation. Plays were signaled in from the sideline as they would be during a game. And Kelly was the one calling the plays.

"His philosophy was, 'If you throw an interception in a game, I'm not going to be there for two or three minutes to tell you what you did wrong,'" Pike said. "'You have to learn how to play the next play. With Mark Dantonio, we would have practices where we're an hour-and-a-half in, and he would re-start the clock because we weren't doing what we needed to do. (Kelly) wanted all of our coaching to be done in the meeting rooms. Then go out on the field, go hard, and go fast for an hour and a half. The players needed to understand how to adjust to this fast tempo. That translated in a lot of ways to what we needed to do in the games."

Off the field, Kelly was a master at dealing with the media, perhaps stemming from his brief career in politics. After he graduated with a bachelor's degree in political science from Assumption College in Worcester, Massachusetts, he spent two years working for state senator Gerry D'Amico, helping D'Amico run Gary Hart's 1984 presidential campaign in Massachusetts. One of his duties was to conduct media briefings. He was a natural.

He knew how to keep his program in the news, a tall order in a city where an NFL team commanded most of the attention in the fall. The Bearcats were never going to receive the blanket coverage that the Bengals got, but if they were going to fill Nippert Stadium they had to find a way to earn a bigger slice of the media pie. Kelly made it part of his mission to make that happen.

The Cincinnati coach saw an early opening in 2007 at the annual Big East Media Day in Providence, Rhode Island, where the league's coaches and athletic directors gathered to promote their product to reporters, columnists and broadcasters from around the conference. He took advantage of it as if he were running back Isaiah Pead bursting through an opening in the offensive line. I was the beat reporter for the Cincinnati Enquirer at the time, but I didn't attend this media day because the paper had decided not to spend the money to send me. In my place, the Enquirer hired a stringer who had covered the Big East for years.

Kelly refused to talk to him, then pointedly criticized the Enquirer in front of the rest of the media for not sending me. He ripped the paper for not serving its readers -- or more importantly in his view -- his program. He knew that if he couldn't get the attention of the largest media outlet in Cincinnati, he would have a hard time getting the program where he wanted to take it.

"I am still going to coach the team and we are still going to compete for a Big East title," Kelly said in Providence. "But it's sad for the fans of Cincinnati to not have a legitimate, credible media outlet. Our fans would be better served going to Rivals, Sporting News, or even the Boston Globe because they are credible sources who care enough about their product to be here."

Later that evening, Kelly was interviewed on Cincinnati radio station WLW-AM, which also failed to send a representative to media day, although he didn't mention that. Instead he ripped the Enquirer again. He told me later that the criticism wasn't directed at me personally, but at the paper, although it sure seemed personal at the time. Since then, the paper has sent a reporter to every conference media day involving local teams. The Enquirer has undergone dramatic changes in the last 10 years, as have most newspapers in America as they're struggled to remain financially viable, but media days have become sacrosanct, even though they rarely generate news of any substance. Credit Kelly for that.

That same year, a few days before the Bearcats were scheduled to play Miami (Ohio) in a rivalry that was more than 100 years old, Kelly floated the idea that it might no longer be worth it for Cincinnati to play its neighborhood rival on an alternating home-and-home basis, intimating that the Bearcats had outgrown the RedHawks because of their recently-acquired status as a BCS school.

"I respect the rivalry and the tradition," Kelly told reporters. "I want to play Miami of Ohio. I think it's great for both institutions anytime you're that close. (But) we're in a BCS conference. We have to look at our schedule and find out, is it in our best interest to travel to a non-BCS school? We have to think about that. That's going to be a decision that's made above my pay grade, but I have my influence in it and I make my opinion known."

That story made the cover of the Enquirer sports section the next day, which was Kelly's goal from the beginning. There was never any intention of altering the series with Miami, Cincinnati officials later told me. And Kelly probably knew that.

The on-field product was different too. The Bearcats could score seemingly on command for their charismatic coach. They were still underdogs, but now they were underdogs with a swagger. The rest of the country didn't yet know how good they were, but they did and that was all that mattered.

As far as Pike is concerned, Kelly was an offensive genius.

"If you look at where we were in the shotgun and no-huddle spread," Pike said, "it was just kind of being introduced to college football. To do what we did and try to get 90 plays in a game had never been done before. He had an answer for everything. That was the genius of Brian Kelly's offense."

Kelce wasn't sure if the genius was solely Kelly's because he didn't want to discount what the rest of the coaching staff did. But he was sure of this much: "We felt like we were always two steps ahead offensively. We were outsmarting the defensive coaches. We were being put in great positions. It's a great feeling as a player. "

Even Gilyard, who remains sharply critical of the way Kelly left in 2009, concedes how much he did for the Cincinnati program.

"What we did in those years under Brian Kelly can't nobody

touch," Gilyard said. "I don't think anybody's ever going to touch it."

4

Unranked

It took Kelly only two years to win a Big East championship at Cincinnati and lead the Bearcats to the Orange Bowl. The breakthrough came in 2008 when they went 11-3 overall, 6-1 in the Big East. They lost in the Orange Bowl to No. 19 Virginia Tech 20-7, but as Kelly pointed out after the game, he viewed that as only the beginning of where Cincinnati football was headed. The Bearcats finished the season with a No. 17 ranking in the Associated Press poll, tying for the highest post-season ranking in school history. Punter Kevin Huber was a first-team All-American and cornerback Mike Mickens was third-team.

Pike started that season as the backup quarterback to Dustin Grutza. After Grutza suffered a broken right leg against No. 4 Oklahoma in the second game of the season, Pike was pressed into action. Finally given the chance to play on a regular basis, he earned second-team All-Big East Conference honors, passing for 2,407 yards and 19 touchdowns.

But none of those 2008 accomplishments seemed to matter when the AP released its preseason rankings for 2009. Despite the return of one of the top quarterbacks in the Big East and eight starters from an offense that averaged 25.9 points and 370 yards, the

Bearcats weren't ranked. Maybe it was because they returned only one starter on defense. Or maybe it was because Cincinnati was still considered a football non-entity nationally and had done nothing to change that thinking with its poor performance in the Orange Bowl.

The Bearcats weren't even picked to repeat as Big East champs, finishing third in the preseason poll of league media behind Pitt and West Virginia.

"It was a shock to us at the time," Pike said. "How are we not preseason ranked? We just used that as at Cincinnati you're not given recognition that maybe you get at a bigger (football) school, the Big Ten or SEC, something like that. It's kind of the Cincinnati way. We don't get the outside recognition. We're going to have to earn everything we get. That carries over in all sports."

That perceived lack of respect was exactly what Kelly was looking for from a motivation standpoint.

"There's things that you say publicly and there's things that you say behind the walls, and that was certainly a great motivator behind the walls," Kelly said. "The one thing we did know was that we were going to score points. And once you know what your weaknesses are, it allows you to do a lot of things to support those. We knew there were some holes (on defense), so we knew how to play. It was pedal to the metal. We're going to outscore you."

Most coaches whose teams have defensive shortcomings play a grind-it-out, ball-control offense to keep the opposing offense -- and by extension their own defense -- off the field. But that wasn't Kelly's style. He decided the Bearcats would play as fast as they could. If that meant the defense spent more time on the field than it would have with a more conventional offensive approach, it also created an aggressive mindset that permeated the team and became its identity.

Kelly was telling the Bearcats' opponents that his offense was so potent they were willing to put their defense in sometimes precarious positions because they knew that ultimately their offense would put enough points on the board to win. The Bearcats played so fast that some defenses gasped trying to keep up.

"We wanted to get after it," Kelly said. "Move fast, think fast, react fast to everything and push it. We needed to be aggressive. That fit who we were from a personality standpoint."

The first chance they had to put their new racecar offense on display came against Rutgers on Labor Day, September 7, in Piscataway, New Jersey. The Scarlet Knights were playing for the first time in newly expanded Rutgers Stadium before a sellout crowd of 53,737. Leading up to the game, Kelly complained about having to play such an important conference game on the road in the first game of the season. But the league, widely considered the weakest of the six BCS conferences, was more than willing to accommodate ESPN's desire for the matchup in return for the national exposure. And despite his grumblings, Kelly also knew that a victory would give his team an early leg up on the rest of the league.

The Scarlet Knights had finished 2008 with seven straight victories, their last loss coming on October 11 against Cincinnati at Nippert Stadium, and they were eager to stop a three-game losing streak against the Bearcats. On defense, Cincinnati was operating under new coordinator Bob Diaco, who switched from a 4-3 alignment to a 3-4, injecting an element of doubt into Rutgers' pre-game preparation because there was no game film to study with the Bearcats playing under their new system.

It took only two minutes, 29 seconds for Cincinnati to score its first touchdown of the season. Pike completed his first six passes for 71 yards, and Pead scored on a two-yard run to give the Bearcats a 7-0 lead. Rutgers came back to tie the score at 7-7 after one quarter. UC then reeled off 38 unanswered points and won, 47-15.

Pike finished with 27 completions in 34 pass attempts for a career-high 362 yards and three touchdowns before leaving the game with 11:25 left in the fourth quarter. Gilyard caught eight passes for 89 yards, Binns caught five for 41, and Woods had four for 71. The UC defense held the Scarlet Knights to 293 yards. Not a bad start for a team that was picked to finish third in the conference.

The Bearcats added a new wrinkle in that game by playing redshirt freshman tight end Travis Kelce at quarterback in their Wildcat formation near the goal line. Kelce, the younger brother of Cincinnati offensive lineman Jason Kelce, was recruited as a quarterback. Kelly wanted to continue to utilize those skills, so he sent Kelce onto the field early in the third quarter and lined him up at quarterback, with Pike shifting to wide receiver. The ball was snapped to Kelce, who ran 12 yards to the Rutgers four-yard line. On the next play, he took another direct snap and scored the first touchdown of his career in his first game. He went on to become one of the best tight ends in Cincinnati history before moving on to an

NFL career with the Kansas City Chiefs, where he became one of the most accomplished tight ends in the league.

"We came out with a fast pace and with a chip on our shoulder," Pike said, "knowing that we had a chance on national TV to show the college football universe what we could do. All of that came together perfectly at Rutgers. After that game, the feeling was that this really can be something special because as a quarterback looking over the weapons we had on offense, you say 'OK, what's a team going to take away? Are they going to try to take away Pead? Then we've got these receivers outside. Are they going to double-team Mardy?' We had an answer for everything. We had Jeff Linkenbach, who went on to play in the NFL, and Jason Kelce, (who became) one of the best centers in the NFL, on the offensive line. So you knew you had the guys up front. It was a good feeling as a quarterback having all those weapons at your disposal."

The win over Rutgers had the feel of a team reaching its peak in the middle of the season instead of an underrated team taking its first halting steps toward proving the naysayers wrong.

"When we beat Rutgers in the fashion that we did, " Gilyard said, "we were like, 'We told you all we were like that.'"

After the lopsided win, it didn't seem to Kelly like such a bad idea to play a key conference game during the first week of the season.

"I knew we were in a really good position," Kelly said, "just getting a feel for our group in that locker room. Just the way they dismantled Rutgers in that game, Kelce coming in at the goal line playing with physicality, I think that kind of set things in motion in the opener."

5

Pike's Awakening

Pike's emergence as one of the best quarterbacks in the country was part of a transformation that began in the summer of 2008, when Kelly approached him in the dining room at Camp Higher Ground in West Harrison, Indiana, early in training camp. By then, Pike had already been at Cincinnati since 2004 and had made zero impact. He had been an outstanding player at Reading High School in an inner ring suburb just northeast of Cincinnati, but he was not heavily recruited despite his obvious physical attributes. His decision to choose Cincinnati over Toledo was an easy one because he grew up a huge Bearcats fan and always wanted to play there. He was a Cincinnati guy through and through.

He was also a classic underachiever. Pike had shown no signs during his first three years that he would amount to anything special even though he stood six-foot-six and had a powerful, accurate arm. He seemed to lack motivation, at times appearing content to linger in the background and let somebody else do the heavy lifting.

Kelly, who took pride in his ability to develop quarterbacks, recognized Pike's potential and was determined to tap into it before it was too late. Pike spent most of the first week of training camp on the sideline watching redshirt freshmen Chazz Anderson and Zach

35

Collaros get the reps he thought should be his as he entered his junior year. That's when Kelly confronted him with a conversation that he calls "blunt and brutally honest."

"We were at a crossroads with a guy that I felt like had an uncanny ability to throw the football at a high percentage," Kelly said. "My job is to get the best version of Tony Pike, to get him to go places that he can't go on his own. Some players don't like it at the time, but when they come back later they thank me. There were a lot of moments where it got personal to the level of 'You've got to step it up or step out.'"

That began a coach-quarterback relationship that Pike describes as "a little jagged from the start."

At the time, 2007 starter Mauk was still involved in an attempt to gain another year of eligibility from the NCAA based on an injury he had suffered at Wake Forest. The NCAA rejected his appeal, leaving the Bearcats' quarterback position unsettled heading into Kelly's second year.

"I think I was sixth on the depth chart," Pike said. "Brian Kelly came up to me and said, 'We're going to give you a chance throughout this camp to show the strides you need to make. If not, we're going to honor your scholarship, but football might not be in your future here at UC.' It wasn't said that nicely. It was more or less 'This is your last chance. 'At the time I was devastated because I loved the game of football, but coming out of that with him, I knew that I would at least get a chance."

Until then, Pike felt that he hadn't been afforded a real

opportunity to show what he could do. He had great respect for Dantonio, but his skills weren't really suited to Dantonio's conservative offense. He realized that Kelly's no-huddle spread offense would suit him much better, but it was up to him to change his approach to the game. By the end of camp he had risen to number two on the depth chart behind Grutza.

"There became an immediate sense of urgency," Kelly said, "and I guess that's what I was looking for more than anything else. Before that, I didn't feel like there was a sense of urgency of him wanting to take his game to the level that it needed to be."

When Grutza was injured in game two against Oklahoma in the third quarter, Pike was ready to seize the moment. He completed only three of 11 passes for 21 yards with one interception against the Sooners. But the following week he made his first career start against Miami (Ohio) and went 20-for-24 for 241 yards with three touchdown passes and no interceptions in a 45-20 Cincinnati rout. He also had five rushes for 33 yards, displaying a surprising ability to run with the ball.

"He was good right away," Kelly said. "A lot of it had to do with his ability to transition into that role in practice. We knew when Dustin went down that we had lost more than just our quarterback. He was a galvanizing player for us with his toughness and spirit and leadership ability. But we knew that Tony would bring another dimension to our offense, and our offense changed to meet what he could do for us."

Pike was a classic pocket passer in contrast to Grutza, who

often improvised on the run. Pike had a stronger arm, better accuracy, and he quickly developed a bond with his receivers, on and off the field.

"He's my brother," Gilyard said. "I don't know how a typical quarterback-receiver relationship would be, but we spent a lot of time together. He knew he could trust me on and off the field. Both of us had a willingness to learn. We wanted to be good. I had never seen anybody throw the ball like that in my life. We just worked and worked and worked.

"(In his first few years at UC) Tony was a product of being too close to home. On weekends, he would go home and eat his mom's cooking. He was like he didn't give a damn. He could hit the eye off a mosquito, then he'd throw five or six passes and you were like, what the hell? That's just how he was. It was mind-boggling. It was like, 'Dude, you can throw like this and you don't give a damn?'"

On September 27, 2008, just as he was beginning to hit his stride, Pike broke his left (non-throwing) arm in the fourth quarter at Akron. By the end of the season, due to injuries, Kelly had been forced to shuffle five different quarterbacks -- Grutza, Pike, Anderson, Collaros and Jones. Grutza and Pike both returned before the season was over, but Pike remained the starter, although Grutza was called on to bail out the Bearcats in a win at Louisville after Pike was forced to leave with a bruised sternum.

Pike was intercepted four times in the Orange Bowl, but he had played well enough during the season to begin 2009 as the

Bearcats' unchallenged starter at quarterback, fully in control of Kelly's high-tech offense.

"We felt like that no team could practice against that," Pike said. "You can't have a scout team in a week that's going to run as fast as we were. Now a defense can't substitute. A defense can't hide blitzes because you're snapping the ball so quick and they can't rotate late. We could either snap the ball really fast or wait and see what the defense was in and then adjust the play."

In 2008, television viewers of Cincinnati games were often treated to the comical sight of Kelly chewing out Pike on the sideline. Pike occasionally tried to explain himself, but was quickly cut off by Kelly and sent on his way. By Pike's senior year theirs was a more collaborative relationship. Kelly still had the last word, though, and still could be seen castigating his quarterback on TV, even though Pike was playing at such a high level.

"Tony was ready when he got the shot and never looked back," Binns said. "He was a guy that towered over the offensive line, who can get the ball to any spot on the field. And the thing about Tony, you can ask anybody who played with him, he's not your typical quarterback as far as his personality. Tony is carefree, a jokester. He's going to make it fun. He's not going to be out there just trying to hammer guys mentally all day. He's going to be out there cracking jokes and having guys relaxed and confident that we're going to move this ball up the field. We're going to do what we do. When you've got a guy that's bringing that confidence to the huddle, it just makes it fun as a receiver."

Brian Kelly frequently castigated Tony Pike on the sideline, but as time passed he became more willing to listen to Pike's side of the story.

Pike and Kelly learned to mesh. Kelly called the plays from the sideline, but Pike had earned the right to change the play at the line of scrimmage based on what he was seeing from the defense.

"My junior year, I felt I had the handcuffs on a little bit, where Coach Kelly would make a lot of the changes," Pike said. "My senior year, I was given the keys to the car a little bit so I could call my audibles. Was he demonstrative on the sideline? Yes? Would he jump down and yell at you? Absolutely. But at the end of the day when you're watching the product on the field you have to respect that 'OK, this guy knows what he's talking about.'"

6

'This Team is a Special Team'

After their season-opening win over Rutgers, the Bearcats moved into the Top 25 for the first time that season at No. 23 as they prepared to return home to face Southeast Missouri State, a Football Championship Subdivision (formerly Division I-AA) school from Cape Girardeau, Missouri. Games against such apparently overmatched opponents, especially early in the season, usually don't amount to much more than an easy win for the home team and a substantial paycheck for the sacrificial lambs. The Bearcats used the mismatch to flex their muscles and continue to build momentum, rolling to a 70-3 victory. Their 67-point margin of victory was the largest for a Cincinnati team since the Bearcats defeated Virginia Military Institute 67-0 in 1953. They were averaging an eye-popping 58.5 points through their first two games.

Gilyard scored four touchdowns in the first half against Southeast Missouri -- one on a punt return, one rushing and two on pass receptions. Redshirt freshman Darrin Williams returned the second-half kickoff 100 yards for a touchdown, and the Cincinnati defense picked off three passes -- one each by Webster, Dominique Battle and linebacker Andre Revels. After the game, Gilyard declared, just two games into the season, "This team is a special team."

"I just saw all this coming together," Gilyard said. "We had all the pieces that we needed. Before the season started, I told the team, 'You all know we have a good chance of going undefeated. You understand that, right?'"

Kelly wouldn't go that far, not yet, but he knew the potential for being special was there. In fact, he had known it since before training camp. Having coached two national championship teams in Division II, he knew special when he saw it.

"This team, more than most teams I've coached, loves to play," Kelly said a few days after the game. "That's a characteristic of great teams that I've had. And I think the skill level is of championship caliber based upon what we looked like last year. We're not there yet, but there's no reason why this team couldn't be there if they continue to do the right things."

The following week, the 17th-ranked Bearcats faced their first ranked opponent of the season when they travelled to Corvallis, Oregon, to take on 2-0 Oregon State, which was ranked 21st in the USA Today coaches poll, but was unranked by the AP. Sean Canfield, the Beavers' quarterback, entered the game leading the nation in completion percentage, having connected on 33 of 42 passes for 78.6 percent, with no interceptions.

Oregon State's Jacquizz Rodgers, a 5-foot-7, 185-pound sophomore running back, was averaging 6.4 yards per carry and 134.5 yards per game with four touchdowns. His brother, James, a junior wide receiver, was closing in on 1,000 career receiving yards.

Two years earlier, the Bearcats had whipped Oregon State, 34-3, at Nippert Stadium, forcing Canfield into three interceptions. But Canfield had grown up considerably, and the Beavers, from the Pac-10 Conference, had a 26-game home winning streak against non-league opponents.

"This is the test," Daniels said before the game. "This is the bump in the road you've got to get over."

The game was played on a balmy, partly sunny afternoon on September 19 at Reser Stadium, before a raucous crowd of 41,909.

"It was one of the loudest places I had ever played," Pike said.

The Bearcats fell behind, 6-0, midway through the first quarter on two field goals by Justin Kahut. Pike's seven-yard touchdown run got them on the board less than a minute into the second quarter, at the end of a nine-play, 80-yard drive that gave Cincinnati a 7-6 lead. After an Oregon State safety, the Bearcats took a 14-8 lead on Pead's one-yard touchdown run. Late in the half, Pike connected with Woods on a 45-yard touchdown pass to provide Cincinnati with a 21-8 halftime lead.

The Beavers came back to get within three points at 21-18 with 13:22 left in the fourth quarter. Gilyard then caught a 19-yard touchdown pass from Pike for the clinching touchdown with 8:03 to play. The Cincinnati defense, which was outstanding the entire game, shut out Oregon State the rest of the way and the Bearcats held on to win, 28-18, improving to 3-0. They had already cleared two crucial hurdles with victories on the road at Rutgers and at

D.J. Woods caught seven passes for 117 yards and a touchdown in the Bearcats' win over Oregon State.

Oregon State.

Receiving a major assist from the defense and having Pike make plays with the game on the line were two more positive signs in a season that was still in its early stages. So was the emergence of Woods, a sophomore wide receiver who caught seven passes for 117 yards and a touchdown against the Beavers, providing the Bearcats with still another offensive weapon. Gilyard (nine catches, 65 yards, one TD) and Binns (six catches, 61 yards) had their usual productive games. And Pike was 31-for-49 for 332 yards with one interception and two touchdowns along with a rare rushing TD.

The Bearcats' confidence in Pike and their offense was growing by the week. As they looked ahead at their schedule, they began to understand that Gilyard's assessment that they could go undefeated might have some merit. There really was no reason why they couldn't run the table. Certainly the talent was there. So was the cutting-edge offense. If the Oregon State players had underestimated them because they were from the Big East, they discovered that Cincinnati was a team to be reckoned with.

"They thought we were going to be a weak team," Gilyard said. "I remember the first kickoff return I had, I got smacked pretty good, but we buckled down and took care of business. We went to the Orange Bowl (in 2008) and they ain't talking about us like they're supposed to. They thought it was a fluke that we went there. But we knew that we could beat them. We knew that we had their number."

Next up was a noon game at Nippert Stadium against Fresno State, a team that appeared perfectly constructed to knock off 14th-ranked Cincinnati.

The Bulldogs, from the Western Athletic Conference, were led by 6-foot, 220-pound junior running back Ryan Mathews, who was leading the nation in rushing with 149 yards per game, averaging 9.1 yards per carry. Cincinnati was ranked fourth nationally in scoring with 48.3 points per game. Fresno State was 20th with 38.7 points per game. The Bearcats had the fifth-ranked passing offense. Fresno State had the fourth-ranked running offense.

Through three games, the Cincinnati defense had allowed an average of only 12 points per game. But with Mathews leading the way and a complementary passing game that produced an average of 212 yards, the defense figured to have its hands full against Fresno State.

"That was a scary football team," Kelly said. "They had one of the best running backs in the country in Ryan Mathews, one of the top offensive lines in the country, and the ability to control the clock."

The Cincinnati defense played without injured starting cornerback Battle. Starting in his place was Marcus (Bones) Barnett, who was moved to defense in 2009 after catching 30 passes for 277 yards and a touchdown as a wide receiver in 2008.

The Bearcats scored first on a 33-yard pass from Pike to Guidugli. Fresno State responded with an 11-play, 55-yard drive that resulted in a 36-yard field goal by Kevin Goessling to make it 7-3. Cincinnati scored again on its second drive, needing only a minute and 43 seconds to go 71 yards in five plays, Pike connecting with

Gilyard for an 11-yard touchdown pass. Rogers' extra point kick gave the Bearcats a 14-3 lead with 5:58 left in the half.

But this would not be another Cincinnati blowout. On their next possession, the Bulldogs went 85 yards in 12 plays, with Mathews scoring from one yard out. Goessling's kick cut Cincinnati's lead to 14-10 with 11:48 remaining in the second quarter. The Bearcats scored again on a one-yard run by Pead to take a 21-10 lead. Fresno State answered with a 17-play, 80-yard drive that consumed eight minutes, 48 seconds and ended with a 21-yard pass from quarterback Ryan Colburn to Jamel Hamler.

At halftime, Cincinnati led 21-17. Mathews had already carried 20 times for 84 yards, an average of 4.2 yards per carry. More ominously, the Bulldogs had the ball for 21 minutes and 20 seconds compared with eight minutes and 40 seconds for Cincinnati.

"This was one of those games where we made a decision to grind it out," Kelly said. "We talked about it on Monday that this is going to be a little bit different, so buckle up, we've got to morph into this game. And we did, and we found a way to win."

There was nothing wrong with the Cincinnati offense, which was humming along as it had been all season. The Bearcats had scored touchdowns on three of their four first-half possessions. But they had run only 25 plays from scrimmage, a long way from the 90 they set as their target for every game.

"It was just, can the defense get enough stops?" Pike said.

That wasn't a given because Mathews was taking a toll on the Bearcats' defense.

"He was a bull," Webster said. "I remember one series where it was almost comical because we knew exactly where they were going. He knew that we knew and they still ran the ball. It was like back-to-back-to-back. I remember during one series I was on the verge of puking because I'm running back and forth trying to hit this guy, then worrying about the linemen coming up. I remember just trying to get him to the ground, trying to hold him up a little bit so I could catch my breath."

None of this surprised Kelly. It didn't take a football genius to know how Fresno State was going to try to beat the Bearcats: Mathews, Mathews and more Mathews.

As the game unfolded, Kelly told defensive coordinator Diaco that his unit had to try to keep the Bulldogs from scoring more than twice. The Bulldogs scored only two touchdowns, both in the second quarter, but bracketed them with two field goals to allow them to remain within striking distance.

The fourth quarter started with the Bulldogs trailing, 21-17, and facing fourth-and-two at the Cincinnati six. But instead of handing the ball to Mathews as they had for most of the game, they decided to fake a handoff up the middle to Mathews and look to pass to the fullback coming out of the backfield. That decision provided Craig Carey with the biggest moment of his Cincinnati career and might have saved the Bearcats' perfect season.

Before going to Cincinnati, Carey had been an outstanding quarterback at Elder High School, a perennial prep football power on the west side of town. As a senior he was named the Offensive

Back of the Year in the Greater Catholic League, one of the premier high school football conferences in the country. He was redshirted as a freshman at Cincinnati in 2005, then played in three games on the kickoff and punt coverage teams the following season.

As a third-year sophomore, he played in all 13 games on special teams, but still saw no action at quarterback, so he was moved to defense for his junior season in 2008 and played 11 games at defensive end. Kelly and his sidekick, strength coach Longo, convinced him to make the switch.

"They talked to me and thought it might be a better situation for me, maybe getting me on the field little bit more," Carey said. "It took a little convincing but I hopped over, went a little harder in the weight room, and added some weight. I ended up playing linebacker and defensive end. It was a little weird. I hadn't played defense since probably the eighth grade. But it ended up working out in our favor."

Moving a quarterback to linebacker, or moving any player to a different position, wasn't an unusual occurrence for Kelly. The best example of a player switching from offense to defense occurred the year before, when Kelly asked tight end Connor Barwin to move to defensive end. Barwin needed some convincing, too, but in the end Kelly's considerable powers of persuasion worked their magic. Barwin went on to lead the Big East in sacks in 2008, was first-team all-Big East, and was drafted in the second round by the Houston Texans. He played for 10 years in the NFL, mostly as an outside linebacker, and made the Pro Bowl in 2014.

This is What the Top Feels Like

Kelly leaned on Longo when he made position changes in an attempt to get his best athletes on the field regardless of which position they were recruited to play. Longo also was in charge of changing the Bearcats' approach in the weight room, especially for the offensive linemen. Because of the conservative run-oriented style that Dantonio favored, the coach liked his linemen big and beefy. For his no-huddle spread, Kelly wanted them to be sleeker and faster.

"He had a similar vision in terms of my background being in Division II," Kelly said of Longo. "We could look at a guy and say, 'Let's not pigeonhole him into a particular position. He can help us somewhere else.' (Longo) was the most important guy on the coaching staff. He was definitely my eyes and ears and was instrumental in everything that we were able to accomplish early on in terms of morale and buy-in."

Carey, a former star quarterback in high school, lined up as an outside linebacker with Fresno State just six yards from the goal line and the victory up for grabs.

"I was watching the fullback and we made eye contact," Carey said. "I remember telling (fellow linebacker) JK Schaffer, 'It's coming to our side.' I was actually blitzing and as I started my assignment I bailed off on the fullback. I guess the quarterback didn't see me. He ended up making that throw and it ended up in my hands. If I had carried out my assignment, there's a good chance they could have scored on that play and we could have lost."

Carey picked off Colburn's pass at the eight and returned his only career interception 21 yards to the Cincinnati 29, where he was stopped by Colburn. The Bearcats needed only six plays to cover 71 yards in a minute and 45 seconds, scoring the clinching touchdown on Pike's 23-yard pass to Gilyard. Rogers' kick gave Cincinnati a 28-17 lead with 13:09 to play.

Criag Carey's interception against Fresno State was one of the biggest defensive plays of the 2009 season.

As the years have passed, Carey's teammates have repeatedly chided him for not returning his interception for a touchdown.

"I think Craig thought he was going to score on that play," said linebacker Andre Revels, one of the team's co-captains. Revels had also played his prep football in Cincinnati, but he played at Colerain, Elder's biggest non-conference rival.

"That Elder speed isn't going to get you in the end zone," Revels said. "If he was in the (Greater Miami Conference) when he played high school ball, he probably would have made that touchdown in college."

"I only had the quarterback to beat," Carey said. "I

definitely should have tried to make him miss and score. Maybe I should have lateraled or something."

Fresno State didn't get past the Cincinnati 30-yard line the rest of the afternoon, but the Bulldogs' Goessling kicked a 49-yard field goal with 8:09 remaining to make the score 28-20. There was still plenty of time for them to score the tying touchdown.

Following a scoreless Cincinnati possession, Rogers pinned Fresno State at its eight-yard line with a 42-yard punt. The Bulldogs then drove to the Bearcats' 33, but on fourth-and-three they were called for delay of game, which pushed them back to the 38. On fourth-and-eight, Colburn's pass, intended for Chastin West, was broken up by Webster. Cincinnati took over on downs with 39 seconds remaining and ran out the clock.

Fresno State had outgained Cincinnati 443 yards to 357, a regular-season low for the Bearcats in 2009. The Bulldogs rushed for 290 yards, 145 of them by Mathews, who carried 38 times. Cincinnati managed only 57 rushing yards and had the ball for 16 minutes and 18 seconds compared with Fresno State's 43 minutes and 42 seconds. In the third quarter, the Bulldogs had the ball for 14 minutes to the Bearcats' one.

But the Cincinnati defense stepped up when the game was on the line, as it did so many times that season.

"When I saw that box score, I realized that a lot of teams lose a game like that," Pike said. "But we took the punches and still found a way to win."

7

'We Just Cared About Winning'

If you were a defensive player on the 2009 Cincinnati football team, you didn't get much time to catch your breath when you came off the field. The offense scored so fast that even after forcing a turnover or a three-and-out, you knew more often than not that you would be back on the field in a matter of minutes. It meant that you played on a team where the offensive stars like Pike and Gilyard attracted most of the attention. The defense was hardly noticed unless it was criticized for not being as good as the offense.

It was hard to blame the defense for feeling as if it were being overlooked. And there were times when the players felt that way. But for the most part, they accepted their supporting roles.

"A lot of attention was on Tony and Mardy," Webster said, "which was deserving, but we had a lot of guys on defense that held their own. They were scoring so fast, we were going back on the field fast, too, so we had to be able to go at the same speed that they were. That's not easy. We felt slighted at times, but we really didn't hold that against our offense. As long as we kept winning like we did, it didn't matter who got the credit. We took it all in stride. It's easy to not worry when you're winning."

The defense was considered the biggest question mark for the

Bearcats when the season began, mostly because Webster, a senior free safety, was the only starter returning from the Orange Bowl team. But Webster never felt like he needed to show the new starters the ropes, because most of them had logged significant playing time the year before.

"Those guys were veterans just like me," Webster said.

Not only did the Bearcats have an almost complete turnover on the starting defensive unit, they were adjusting to a new coordinator and a new system. Diaco had replaced Joe Tresey after Tresey was fired over philosophical differences with Kelly, following a season in which the Bearcats were ranked 31st nationally in total defense.

First-year defensive coordinator presided over a switch from a 4-3 alignment to a 3-4.

As a player, the 36-year-old Diaco had been a two-time all-Big Ten selection at Iowa and a semifinalist for the Butkus Award that goes to the nation's top linebacker. Kelly lured him away from Virginia, where he had just been named defensive coordinator after three years of coaching linebackers and special teams under Al Groh. Getting the chance to work under Kelly was the main reason Diaco took the Cincinnati job. He had worked under Kelly at Central Michigan and relished the opportunity to do it again because he knew Kelly would allow him to "put into action some of the thoughts that I had developed about defending."

With the new 3-4 system, the lack of returning starters actually worked to Diaco's advantage because nearly everyone was starting over together.

"It was a big change," Diaco said. "And they did a beautiful job with it. They cared a great deal and put in the extra work. They were an impressive group of guys. Everybody started fresh. Everybody was wide open to learning from each other, including myself."

The Bearcats' defense wasn't lacking in talent. Webster was a first-team all-Big East selection in 2009. Defensive lineman Derek Wolfe was a sophomore who became a starter, and developed into a second-team All-American and first-team all-Big East selection as a senior. He was a second-round pick by the Denver Broncos, and he was still playing in the NFL in 2019.

Defensive lineman John Hughes was the Cleveland Browns' third-round pick in 2012. And defensive lineman Ricardo Mathews was a seventh-round pick of the Indianapolis Colts. Linebackers Curtis Young and sophomore JK Schaffer, a local product from La Salle High School, both played in the NFL. Strong safety Drew Frey, who was a redshirt freshman on the 2009 team, developed into a first-team all-Big East player in 2011.

"We never got credit because the defense was a bend-but-don't-break defense, but our defense was loaded too," Daniels said.

Diaco points to Webster, Mathews, Daniels and Schaffer as strong leaders on the defensive unit, even though Schaffer was only a sophomore.

"He led by example," Diaco said of Schaffer. "He worked his tail off. He was just a quiet, 'Hey, follow me, do what I do' kind of guy. He was one of the hardest workers on the team, and he made a lot of plays for us that year."

Revels was the heart and soul of the unit. He played in 13 games as a junior and was getting the chance to start for the first time as a senior. He ended up leading the Bearcats in tackles with 108, but most fans had no idea what he had to go through just to get on the field every day.

A first-team all-Ohio player who helped lead Cincinnati's Colerain High School to the 2004 Ohio Division I state championship, Revels had knee surgery in high school, the result of a torn lateral meniscus injury to his left knee that he suffered while playing on the punt return team.

"As the whistle was blown, a guy came up from behind me and dove directly at my leg," Revels recalled. "I think it was probably a pretty dirty play. I remember watching the film of that. I wanted to punch that guy in the face as the game was going on, but I wasn't going to get the penalty. He tried to take my knee out from under me."

Including the surgery he had at Colerain, Revels had a total of three operations on the knee. After the third, in January 2009, veteran trainer Bob Mangine cautioned Revels that he might not be able to play football again. Revels refused to accept that as even a remote possibility and spent an average of two to three hours every day receiving treatment, more than any player Mangine had ever worked with.

"It's one of those things where, when you're focused on a goal, the obstacles always seem surmountable," Revels said. "Having to put in additional time for treatment or having to alter the way you practice or the way you approach the game is just another thing that you do in order to accomplish the goal. So I didn't see it as a hindrance. I didn't see that it was very much outside of just another thing like weightlifting or film watching that was going to help me accomplish my goal every day."

Despite all he was going through just to get on the field, Revels rarely, if ever, talked about it.

"He was a in a great deal of pain and adversity every single week with his knee," Diaco said. "He just quietly went through a process that most people wouldn't even dream of doing. That thing was in bad shape, and he gutted it out for the team, so it was easy to follow him, even myself. It was easy to be energized by what he was going through. It was real, too. I watched it."

Kelly has never forgotten Revels' dedication and what it meant to that team. A few years ago, Revels was with his girlfriend, now his wife, as spectators at the Pebble Beach Pro-Am golf tournament in Pebble Beach, California when Kelly, one of the participants, hit a ball near the fence where Revels was standing.

"He came over and he looked up and saw me," Revels said. "He came right over to me and said, 'Hey, Andre.' I hadn't talked to him in four or five years and he knew my face and everything. At the pro-ams you're not supposed to stop play. You're not supposed to take pictures. He came outside the gate to the roped-off area and took a picture with me and then he continued

Linebacker Andre Revels poses with Brian Kelly at the Pebble Beach Pro-Am golf tournament. *Photo courtesy of Andre Revels*

playing. That's the type of guy that Brian Kelly is.

"When he stopped, the security guard was like, 'Hey, you need to move along.' Brian was like, 'This is one of my guys who made me who I am and helped me get where I am. I can take a few seconds to take this picture right now.' When you have that type of brotherhood and you play with one goal like we did in college, to see somebody years down the road, when you haven't talked to them or spoken their name or anything, and they see you and it's an instant recollection, that feels good. He's coached first-round linebackers in the (NFL), and I'm not that. For him to have that kind of rapport with me, that's pretty special. That's a tribute to him and how he actually feels about his players."

When I mentioned the Pebble Beach encounter to Kelly, he remembered it immediately.

"Andre Revels was a warrior," Kelly said. "He played that entire season with a bad knee, maybe a knee that you shouldn't play with, and I respected the heck out of his commitment to our football team. That's why that team meant so much to me, because it was made up of such different personalities. He was a throwback player."

The irrepressible Revels paid no attention to what outsiders were saying about the Cincinnati defense. In fact, he said, the ability to tune that stuff out contributed to its success. Revels started at inside linebacker alongside Schaffer. Young and Walter Stewart started on the outside. By the end of the season, Wolfe, Mathews, and Daniels were starting on the defensive line, with Brad Jones and Dominique Battle at the corners. Webster started at free safety and Drew Frey at strong safety.

The Cincinnati defense allowed 23.1 points per game in 2009, which ranked fifth among the eight Big East teams; and 374 yards per game, which ranked last. The Bearcats were 44th out of 120 Football Bowl Subdivision teams in average points allowed. Those numbers paled in comparison to the gaudy numbers the offense put up week after week to rank fourth nationally with an average of 38.6 points. The offense scored so fast its average scoring drive was just two minutes, twenty-six seconds. That kept the Cincinnati defense on its toes.

"We just had this attitude of being ready for sudden change because our offense was a quick-striking, faster-tempo, gun-it style of offense," Frey said..

Frey understood why the defense was often overlooked, at times even criticized. "Part of playing at that level is to kind of ignore the noise, but there's always criticism," he said. "As long as we got the victory at the end of the game, that was the most important part. But we definitely played with a chip on our shoulder. With the culture that we developed, we played until the whistle. We never gave up, no matter the circumstances."

Frey was an offensive star at Clinton-Massie High School in nearby Clinton County. He was another local product on a team that had 30 players from Greater Cincinnati, many of whom were walk-ons. During his final two years of high school, he combined for 3,455 yards rushing and receiving. He ran for 1,493 yards as a senior, and 1,574 yards as a junior. He also won state titles in the long jump and as a member of the 4x100 relay team.

Despite those impressive credentials -- he was also his class valedictorian -- Cincinnati was the only Division I school to offer him a scholarship. Frey was one of many players on the 2009 team who were not high-level recruits. Others were high-level recruits who didn't live up to their rankings at other schools and were looking for a fresh start.

Strong safety Drew Frey was one of many Cincinnati players who weren't heavily recruited out of high school.

One such player was Demetrius Jones, considered one of the top quarterbacks in the country coming out of high school. He signed with Notre Dame, but when things didn't work out with the Fighting Irish he transferred to Cincinnati. His decision to leave Notre Dame put the Bearcats in the national news, where historically they had spent very little time.

But when Jones got to Cincinnati, the medical staff found that he needed surgery for a torn labrum. After the surgery, his throwing motion was never the same. So, in another attempt to get his best athletes on the field regardless of position, Kelly moved Jones to linebacker. Jones accepted the move, but never relinquished his desire to be a quarterback.

When I interviewed him during spring practice in April,

shortly after the move was made, Jones surprised me when he said "This is something temporary for me. Depending on how the spring goes and how stuff works over on offense, that's what I'll be basing my next move on. I know I can play quarterback. At the same time, I know I'm an athlete. I'm fast and there's other things that I can do."

Kelly's response?

"He's playing defense. His only other option would be to play another sport. I don't think he wants to play another sport. I

think he wants to play football."

So Jones played defense. And he played on special teams. And he made the key block that helped pave the way for Gilyard's game-changing kickoff return against Pittsburgh.

Demetrius Jones started his college career as a quarterback at Notre Dame. He ended up playing linebacker at Cincinnati.

The Cincinnati defense had the advantage -- and the misfortune -- of practicing every day against one of the most potent offenses in the country, an offense that operated at a tempo few others could match.

"It was fun defensively because you got to fly around the

field," Revels said. "Everyone remembered our offense, but our defense was a brotherhood. There was communication at all levels, from the DBs and linebackers to the line. We played in some really loud environments, so we had a lot of hand signals and a lot of unspoken communication. That's a tribute to Aaron Webster and the DBs. Myself and JK Schaffer, we could just look at each other and know exactly what play we were going to adjust to. The defensive line was very receptive to those changes at a moment's notice to be able to put themselves in the right position."

When Webster lined up against the Bearcats' offense in practice, the play was so intense he felt like he was playing in a regular-season game.

"It was almost not fair," Webster said, "because they would have a script, so they would know the plays they were running in five-play increments. But that offense definitely got us prepared for games, that's for sure."

At times, Webster actually felt sorry for the opposing defense as he watched it try to stop Cincinnati's offense, "especially when Mardy or D.J. would make a play, or even Isaiah. That's a tough position to be in. Those guys were track-fast. They were literally running past people."

There's no disputing that the Cincinnati defense wasn't as good statistically as the offense. Perhaps that would have been too much to ask. But the 2009 Bearcats didn't win with offense alone. Their defense was solid when it needed to be. So were their special teams.

"We were playing complementary football by design to be sure we ended up with one more point than our opponent," Diaco said. "I don't get caught up with statistics. I just want to look at the game and be able to maneuver tactically as the game is unfolding to be sure you're fitting in with the other two phases to have more points. That was obvious and I think the people saw it. The people who cared about the program saw it for exactly what it was.

"It was a keep-the-points-down group. Force them to execute. There's no need to be overly aggressive. If our offense is getting enough possessions, then we're OK. And we were. We got enough stops, forced field goals, and we were scoring touchdowns. We had a real nice recipe for winning."

Cincinnati's offensive players knew how much the defense meant to the entire team, even if it didn't always shine. Pike, for one, understood how difficult it must have been for his defensive teammates playing on the same team with such a prolific offense.

"Our defense for a lot of the year was criticized for giving up a lot of points," Pike said. "Maybe they weren't making plays for four quarters, but our defense stepped up when we needed them. That's what made the team so good. When the offense was rolling, the defense could maybe get away with having a bad series. And when the offense struggled, the defense made big plays when we needed them."

In some ways, playing defense on the 2009 Cincinnati football team must have been like being a pitcher on baseball's Big Red Machine. Everyone remembers the great offensive players, but the pitchers were effective too. What mattered was that those Cincinnati Reds teams won back-to-back World Series championships in 1975 and 1976 and are considered one of the great dynasties in major league history.

"We were so talented and so good, we just cared about winning," Carey said. "The public perception about being an offensive juggernaut was fine. I guess that puts people in the stands."

Spotlight

'We Needed a Cincinnati Flavor'

For 16 years, Kerry Coombs was content as the head football coach at Colerain High School in suburban Cincinnati. Coombs had built the Cardinals into one of the top prep powers in the state of Ohio. Ten of his teams qualified for the playoffs with seven undefeated regular seasons. At Colerain, he coached Revels, along with Terrill Byrd, who became an All-American defensive lineman at Cincinnati, and Dominick Goodman, who became one of the top receivers in Bearcats history.

When Kelly decided that he needed a Cincinnati flavor on his coaching staff, he turned to Coombs in a surprise move, hiring him as associate head coach and defensive secondary coach, with the understanding that Coombs could help the Bearcats succeed in recruiting top local prep players.

Coombs was a walking bundle of intensity, chatter and enthusiasm. When one of his players intercepted a pass, Coombs would get so excited he'd sprint down the sideline pumping his fist and jumping up and down like a little kid. If you didn't know better, you'd think he was the one who had picked off the pass. This might have come off as high school stuff, but it was genuine with Coombs. He saw no reason to tone things down just because he was coaching in college. That just wouldn't be him.

Even with no college coaching experience and no previous relationship with Kelly, hiring Coombs' made perfect sense to the new Cincinnati head coach.

"I believed that we needed a Cincinnati tattoo on our arm and there wasn't one more emblematic of that than Kerry Coombs," Kelly said. "We needed a Cincinnati flavor, plus he was a damn good football coach. I wanted to be around good people, too, putting a staff together. He checked all those boxes. He had great enthusiasm and great passion and still has it today."

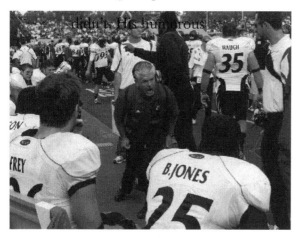

Former Colerain High School coach Kerry Coombs provided the Bearcats with a Cincinnati flavor and a heavy dose of intensity.

Coombs jumped in with both feet. He was a constant vocal presence during practice, peppering his charges with praise when they played well and with criticism when they didn't. His humorous -- and often cutting -- comments were frequently the most entertaining part of practice.

"I don't know how long he'd been hired when he called me," Coombs said of Kelly. "It was pretty early on, December 16 (2006) or something like that. It wasn't something I was really looking to do. I loved my job. He called me on a Thursday and I met with him on Friday. My wife and I decided to take it on Saturday. On Monday we had a team meeting at 6:30 in the morning. and we were in bowl game prep."

The Bearcats had earned the right to play against Western Michigan in the International Bowl in Toronto. Kelly agreed to coach the Bearcats in the bowl game after Dantonio, who had been the Bearcats' head coach during the regular season, left for Michigan State.

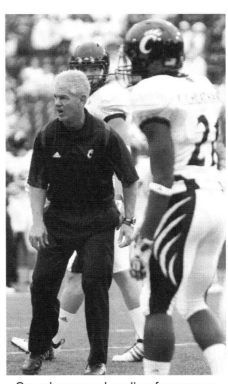
Coombs was a bundle of energy on the sideline during games.

"We were having to coach off the old playbook," Coombs said. "The players knew the playbook, not the coaches. It would have been unfair for us to try to change anything."

With Kelly running the show, the Bearcats defeated Western Michigan 27-24. Central Michigan, the team Kelly had just left, knocked off Middle Tennessee in the Motor City Bowl in Detroit. Kelly had left a few members of his staff behind to coach the Chippewas.

As soon as the bowl games were over, Kelly -- with help from the rah-rah Coombs -- got down to the business of building his new program and expanding the Cincinnati fan base.

"Mark left a good team," Coombs said. "We had talented players, but people weren't overly excited. The crowds weren't probably what they ought to be. (Kelly) went to work developing an attitude and trying to sell tickets, and he was wonderful at it. Brian and I were doing these little community get-togethers at bars and restaurants, talking to anybody who would listen to us."

As he looks back on Cincinnati's 2009 season, Coombs doesn't see a defense that had to take a back seat to anybody, regardless of how potent the offense was. He's proud of the work that unit contributed to the undefeated season.

"When you coached with Brian you understood that his passion was always going to be offense," Coombs said. "He was going to score. The greatest thing in the world is to be a defensive coach knowing that your offense is going to score. We were never out of reach in any game. But I don't think the defense was bad. The defense was extremely competitive."

Coombs left Cincinnati in 2012 to coach under Urban Meyer at Ohio State. After six seasons with the Buckeyes, he was hired as the secondary coach for the NFL Tennessee Titans. But he still thinks of himself as a high school coach.

"I owe an awful lot to Brian Kelly," Coombs said. "I tell people all the time I'm just a high school football coach. He changed my life."

8

New Twist to an Ancient Rivalry

On October 3, in Cincinnati's first game following its win over Fresno State, the Bearcats' defense delivered again this time against long-time rival Miami (Ohio), making another big play when the game was on the line. Cincinnati pressured Miami quarterback Zac Dysert, a redshirt freshman who was making just his second career start, into 10 sacks, taking advantage of an inexperienced offensive line. The defense also forced Dysert into two interceptions, although he did throw for 286 yards and a touchdown.

"That game is when we all came together," Daniels said.

Cincinnati and Miami, located only 40 miles apart, first played football against each other on Dec. 8, 1888, when they grappled to a scoreless tie in Oxford, Ohio. It was the first college football game played in Ohio, one month after Benjamin Harrison defeated Grover Cleveland to become the 23rd U.S. president.

The Battle for the Victory Bell is loaded with colorful history. It's the oldest rivalry in the country between two schools from different conferences and ranks fifth among the longest-running rivalries in college football. The original bell hung in Miami's Harrison Hall and was used to celebrate Miami victories. The current trophy is a replica of the original bell. The winning team gets to keep the bell for a year until the next game in the rivalry. When Cincinnati has it, the players tote it out to practice in the days leading up the Miami game. They display it in the football offices during that week. And they ring it every chance they get.

Jimmy Nippert, after whom Cincinnati's Nippert Stadium is named, suffered a spike wound in the 1923 game against Miami and died a month later from blood poisoning. His grandfather, James N. Gamble, one of the founders of Cincinnati-based Procter & Gamble, donated the money to complete the horseshoe-shaped stadium as a memorial to Jimmy.

Under Brian Kelly, Cincinnati went 3-0 in the annual Battle for the Victory Bell against rival Miami (Ohio).

Despite all that history, when the 4-0 Bearcats made the short bus ride up U.S. 27 to Oxford on October 3, 2009, the rivalry had a new twist. The Bearcats had never faced their neighborhood rival as a Top 10 team. In fact, Cincinnati had never played anyone as a Top 10 team, which it became when it checked in at No. 10 in the AP poll following its September 26 win over Fresno State. Miami had never hosted a Top 10 team.

The rivalry had long been dominated by Miami, which held a 59-48-7 advantage and had won four of the last five games. But under Kelly, the Bearcats had blown out the RedHawks in their last two meetings -- 47-10 in 2007 and 45-20 in 2008. Cincinnati and had won the last three games. Miami, which was playing its first home game at Yager Stadium under first-year head coach Mike Haywood, had lost nine straight games overall, including its last five in 2008 and its first four in 2009. The Bearcats were seeking their first four-game winning streak in the rivalry since 1989.

The Miami game was always special to Pike, who was recruited by the RedHawks out of high school. He made his first career start against Miami in 2008, passing for 245 yards and three touchdowns in a Cincinnati win.

"Miami had recruited me a lot and then kind of disappeared at the last minute," Pike said. "But once UC offered, it wouldn't have mattered where I was offered, I was going to go to UC. I grew up a huge UC fan, being from Cincinnati. But at the time, I thought it would be Toledo or Miami, and Miami was more pass-happy coming off the (Ben) Roethlisberger era, so it would have been a better fit than Toledo."

A crowd of 23,493 gathered for the 1 p.m. kickoff. Miami fans were encouraged to wear white or, as school officials not so cleverly put it, "Do the white thing," to encourage the RedHawks to pull off what would have been one of the greatest upsets in the history of the rivalry.

On paper, the game was so lopsided it was hard to imagine

When Jacob Ramsey rushed for 103 yards against Miami, he became the first Cincinnati player to gain 100 yards in a game since Butler Benton in gained 101 against Southeastern Missouri State in 2007.

an upset. The Bearcats were ranked fifth nationally in scoring offense, averaging 43.2 points per game. Miami, which started four freshmen on defense -- three on the defensive line -- was ranked 119th in scoring defense, allowing 41.8 points per game. Those Miami numbers gave Pike another reason to look forward to renewing the rivalry.

On a seasonably cool, gray and windy Saturday. Cincinnati led, 23-7, at halftime. Two of its three touchdowns were set up by Miami mistakes. With the Bearcats leading, 6-0, on the strength of the first of three Jacob Ramsey rushing touchdowns, Miami punter Chris DiCesare's six-yard punt gave the Bearcats possession on the

Miami 42. The RedHawks appeared to have stopped the Cincinnati offense on its next possession, but when the Bearcats lined up to punt, Miami was whistled for an illegal substitution penalty. That prompted Kelly to go for the big play. On fourth-and-three from the Miami 35-yard line, Pike connected with Binns for a touchdown pass to give the Bearcats a 13-0 lead.

On Miami's next possession, Haywood called for a fake punt on fourth-and-one, but Austin Moore was stopped short of the first down by Cincinnati's Charley Howard and Obadiah Cheatham. The Bearcats took over on the Miami 27. Pike threw to Binns for 13 yards, Ramsey ran around the right end for six, then up the middle for eight more and a touchdown. Rogers' extra point kick put Cincinnati ahead 20-0. Miami's only touchdown of the half came on a one-yard run by Thomas Merriweather Jr., but that was partially negated by Rogers' 42-yard field goal.

Somehow the RedHawks found a way to make a game of it despite being so decidedly outmanned. Following a 19-yard touchdown pass from Dysert to Andre Bratton, they went for two and appeared to have made it, but the conversion was wiped out by an offensive pass interference penalty. Forced to kick from 25 yards away, Trevor Cook missed the extra point, leaving the score at 23-13 with five minutes left in the third quarter. The RedHawks then surprised Cincinnati with an onside kick that Miami's Anthony Kokal recovered at the Cincinnati 45. The RedHawks were still very much in the game.

That's when the Cincinnati defense stepped up. Miami drove

Linebacker JK Schaffer stops a Miami rally with an interception in the end zone.

to the Cincinnati three-yard line, where on third-and-goal, just when it appeared as if the RedHawks were about to pull within three points of the Bearcats, Schaffer was in the right place at the right time. Dysert slipped as he attempted a pass, and Schaffer picked it off in the end zone, returning it to the Cincinnati 13-yard line. It was the biggest defensive play of the game, and one the Bearcats sorely needed to keep their rivals at bay.

The final score was a convincing 37-13, which extended the Bearcats' record to 5-0. Cincinnati gained 434 yards. Pike passed for 270 yards and two touchdowns, and Ramsey rushed for 103 yards.

But Kelly wasn't impressed by the way his team had played. He said after the game that the Bearcats had won despite not bringing their 'A' game.

That may have been true, but it was definitely a day to remember for Ramsey, who became the first Cincinnati back to rush for 100 yards in a game since Butler Benton gained 101 against Southeast Missouri State on August 30, 2007. It was a rare moment in the spotlight for Ramsey, a senior from Columbus who went about his business in a quiet, unassuming manner. He wasn't an electrifying back by any stretch of the imagination, and his role in Kelly's spread offense didn't afford him many chances to shine.

As a junior, he led the Bearcats in rushing with 664 yards on 152 carries, for 47.4 yards per game, 3.8 yards per carry. He shared the workload almost equally with fellow junior John Goebel, who carried 133 times for 607 yards. Goebel was limited by a hamstring injury in 2009, but Ramsey still had to share the wealth, this time with up-and-coming sophomore Pead, who was on his way to becoming one of the best running backs in school history.

By the end of the season, Pead had become the featured back, but Ramsey never complained.

"Pead was a young player and Jacob was a seasoned veteran player, a really good leader on our football team," Kelly said "For us to supplant him it would require Isaiah to show consistency in everything he did. And that's what we saw that year (in Pead). He was a guy that was on top of his game, on top of what he was doing assignment-wise, taking care of the little things."

Pead finished the season with 806 yards on 121 carries with nine touchdowns and a 6.7-yard per carry average. Ramsey carried 74 times for 439 yards and four touchdowns with a 5.9-yard per carry average, not a bad one-two rushing combination for a passing team.

"We could run the football," Kelly said proudly, as if to dispel the notion that all the Bearcats could do was pass.

The Miami game might have been even more meaningful to Daniels, the defensive end who had four of the Bearcats' 10 sacks against the RedHawks. He had almost seen his college football career come to an end due to an incident that occurred while he was playing at Minnesota, where he was one of four players dismissed from the team.

According to a July 18, 2007 Associated Press story, Minnesota junior Dominic Jones was accused of having sex with an 18-year-old woman who was "physically helpless" after a night of binge drinking at a campus apartment in April of the same year. Investigators said Daniels used his cell phone to video Jones having sex with the woman. The county attorney said that Daniels and two other Minnesota players also had sex with the woman earlier that night, but Daniels was not charged with a crime.

Daniels had no place to go until he got a reprieve from Kelly and the Cincinnati administration. But Kelly made him earn his second chance.

"I was an immature kid," Daniels said. "And then I had to grow up. Coach Kelly turned me into a man. He said, 'Either you're going to do what I'm telling you to do or you're never going to play football again.' When I first came to Cincinnati, Coach Kelly kicked me out of his office three times."

The first thing Daniels was required to do on his road back to football was get his academic affairs in order. He started out by going to Cincinnati's Blue Ash College and posted a paltry 0.9 grade point average.

"I was travelling from Columbus to Cincinnati every day because I didn't have the money to pay for housing and books," Daniels said. "Coach Kelly kicked me out of the office. He said, 'I can't help you.' I tried to explain my situation to him, and he didn't care. I understand now why he did that. He wanted to see if I wanted it as bad as I said I did. I had to take out a loan to pay for my books and my housing. I ended up with a 3.6 the next quarter and made the Dean's List. I went back to his office and he said, 'This is what I'm talking about. I can take this to the president (Nancy Zimpher).'

"He took it to her and she denied it, so I had to go back to Blue Ash for another quarter. I got a 3.8 this time. I had just torn my Achilles tendon in the weight room. So now I don't have no football team, I have no money, I have no food. I was staying in Jacob Ramsey's room when I first got there. Then once I got to be part of the team I had to take so many classes just to get eligible to get a scholarship. I had to take 16 hours in the summer."

After he became eligible, Daniels backed up Lamonte Nelms in 2008. He didn't start in the 2009 season opener against Rutgers, but he still managed seven tackles and a sack coming off the bench. He became a fixture in the starting lineup beginning with week two against Southeast Missouri State, and finished the season with two sacks against Florida in the Sugar Bowl. For the season, he led the Bearcats with 8.5 sacks and was tied with Curtis Young for second in tackles for loss (11.0) behind Ricardo Mathews (12.5).

"He was highly skilled, was committed to the craft, and held the younger guys accountable as an experienced person," Diaco said of Daniels. "He had experienced all of the good and all of the bad as it relates to growing up. He was willing to lead and he was willing to share. He was a real source of energy and checks and balances on the sideline during the game. I loved being on a team with him."

Daniels wasn't drafted and never played in an NFL game, but he spent time with the Oakland Raiders, Dallas Cowboys and New Orleans Saints on either their off-season roster or their practice squad.

"That season was the most important football season to me in my life," Daniels said, "because it was the last chance I had to even smell a chance to go to the NFL. I played hard on every play. I never took a play off because I never knew when it was going to be my last."

Spotlight

Pike for Heisman

By the second week of October, Pike's national profile had risen to the point where ESPN.com rated him behind Florida's Tim Tebow, Texas' Colt McCoy and Notre Dame's Jimmy Claussen on a list of leading contenders for the Heisman Trophy, which annually goes to the nation's top college football player.

"It came out of nowhere," Pike said.

At that point, Pike had passed for 1,493 yards and 13 touchdowns, with just three interceptions, while completing 66.7 percent of his passes.

Pike couldn't believe how his life had changed. Just a few years earlier, his college career appeared to be going nowhere. Now he was a star in his hometown, for the college football team he rooted for growing up, and was considered a legitimate Heisman Trophy candidate. It was almost too good to be true.

"I was just trying to be the general of the team, understanding that I didn't have to do everything." Pike said. "The Heisman stuff, if you let yourself get engulfed in it, it starts affecting your play. If you're in the third quarter, you might be thinking, 'OK, I need to throw some touchdowns.' I was having fun doing what I loved to do for a city and a school that I loved, so anything that came on top of that was a bonus."

While Pike tried to take the recognition in stride, one Cincinnati media personality eagerly embraced the concept of Pike for the Heisman. Mo Egger had a daily sportstalk show on WCKY-AM radio and was the engineer for the radio broadcasts of Cincinnati's games on WLW-AM. He was also involved on the air with pre-game and post-game programming of Bearcat football games. He first saw Pike mentioned as a Heisman candidate after the Cincinnati's season-opening win against Rutgers when the subject was broached in a game story written by Mike Freeman of CBS Sports.

A few weeks later, as the Bearcats kept winning and Pike continued to excel, Egger sensed that this could be a landmark season for the Bearcats and that maybe, just maybe, Pike really could win the Heisman.

Cincinnati has never had a Heisman Trophy winner. In fact, up to this point, it had never even had a true Heisman candidate, even though the Bearcats have had some fine quarterbacks: Greg Cook, who played for Cincinnati from 1966-68, went on to become Rookie of the Year in the old American Football League before his career was cut short by shoulder problems; and Gino Guidugli, the brother of Cincinnati tight end Ben Guidugli, who still held many of the Bearcats' school passing records from an outstanding career that spanned from 2001 to 2004.

The only other time the school had attempted to openly promote one of its players as a Heisman candidate was in 1987, when it put quarterback Danny McCoin on the cover of its football media guide and ballyhooed him for the award. That idea went nowhere.

Egger looked around and saw how other schools promoted their Heisman candidates and figured he would have a go at it himself.

"I thought, 'Wouldn't it be cool if that kind of thing happened for Tony?'" Egger said. "I just thought it would be fun to have a Cincinnati kid playing for a Cincinnati school in that conversation. I thought, 'If this kid continues to play like he is, who's to say he can't get to New York (as a finalist)?' I remember thinking that somebody should undertake this effort. It should have come from the school, but if it didn't, why not me?"

Radio personality Mo Egger sold these T-shirts to promote Tony Pike for the Heisman Trophy. *Photo courtesy of Dan Hoard.*

Egger's motives weren't entirely selfless. It's true that he believed such a campaign would be good for the school and for Pike. But he also figured it would create attention for him.

At the time, Egger -- who now does his own show every afternoon on Cincinnati's WCKY-AM -- was just starting out as a talk show host. He had hosted a morning show that, by his own estimation, wasn't very good, and he had recently moved to the afternoon, so he was looking for all the publicity he could get. With a friend's help, he decided to design and sell "Pike for Heisman" T-shirts and donate any money he made to charity.

"I thought if it snowballed, people would really get excited," Egger said. "It felt kind of grass roots. I just thought it could be a fun aspect for a fun part of a season that looked like it could be really, really good. We had a 'Pike for Heisman' web site. We thought we'd sell them for 20 or 25 bucks."

Egger had just gotten his promotional venture off the ground when he received a phone call from Cincinnati associate sports information director Ryan Koslen.

"He says, 'Hey, you're going to make Tony ineligible for the game this week,'" Egger said. "'Under NCAA rules, you can't use his likeness to make a profit. You can't sell a student-athlete's name or likeness. He'll pay the price.' I didn't want to upset the school, and I didn't want to affect Tony, and I didn't want Brian Kelly to never come on my show again. So we quickly stopped selling the T-shirts. I don't know how many we sold, maybe a couple dozen. A couple days later, I got a cease-and-desist order from the Heisman Trophy trust from using the name Heisman for my own profit."

That was the end of the 'Pike for Heisman' campaign. It was an unfortunate turn of events for a well-intentioned endeavor, but as it turned out, it would have ended the following week anyway, when Pike suffered a serious injury playing at South Florida that caused him to miss three games and parts of two others. As a result, we'll never know if Pike actually would have had a legitimate shot at the

Heisman. Because Cincinnati was not a big-time football school well known by Heisman voters, it seemed unlikely. But it's fun to think about, even 10 years later.

"Would I have won it?" Pike said. "I don't know. If things would have played out and I had stayed healthy, I think I would have been in New York for it because I think we would have continued the success we were having."

Egger doesn't have one of the Pike T-shirts. He's looked online to see if anyone might be selling one, but hasn't had any luck. Pike has one, though, because his family bought some before they were outlawed. But he says he never wears it.

Today Pike and Egger are close friends. They do a show together weekdays at noon called "Cincy 360" on the same station where Egger does his show. But in 2009, Pike knew Egger only as the guy who did the pre-game and post-game shows on the radio. And he didn't appreciate what Egger said after he threw four interceptions against Virginia Tech in the Orange Bowl at the end of the 2008 season.

"After the game, Mo signed off with, 'On a night where Tony Pike became more like Tony Pick,'" Pike said. "At the time I was like, I don't know if I like this guy very much."

9

Pead and the Bearcats Rule Ohio

The day after the Bearcats knocked off Miami, the new AP rankings came out and there it was in black and white -- another rarity for Cincinnati -- the Bearcats were ranked ahead of Ohio State.

The 5-0 Bearcats jumped from No. 10 to No. 8, climbing past the 4-1 Buckeyes, something that just isn't supposed to happen in Ohio. In fact, no Ohio school had been ranked higher than Ohio State since 2004, when Bowling Green was ranked 25th in a week when the Buckeyes were unranked. The last time Cincinnati had been ranked ahead of Ohio State was November 21, 1951.

To celebrate their new superiority, Cincinnati fans started to wear black T-shirts that read, 'BUCKEYE STATE," with the letters 'UC' and 'STATE' in white over red letters. The 'C' in 'UC' was in the form of the Cincinnati C-paw logo, signifying that the Bearcats, however temporarily, now owned the state when it came to college football. Never mind that Ohio State had eight national championships and seven Heisman Trophy winners -- tied for the most in the country -- to none and none for Cincinnati. It was only the moment that mattered. And for now the Bearcats ruled.

The shirt could have been designed specifically for Pead, who

When the Bearcats landed in the AP Top 10, they were ranked ahead of Ohio State for the first time since 1951.

grew up in Columbus hoping to play for Ohio State. That didn't work out, mostly due to Pead's poor academic record in high school, although he had no assurance that the Buckeyes would have offered him a scholarship even if he had been a standout student. It didn't matter now, because he was starring for a Cincinnati team that was ranked higher than his once-beloved Buckeyes.

"That was sweet," Pead said. "Believe me, everybody back home, even now, all my friends and family are big Buckeye fans. It was a great time for me with bragging rights, that we were no longer the little brothers."

Pead lived with his mother and his grandparents when he was growing up. Just outside Pead's bedroom in the basement, his grandfather had an Ohio State room complete with a Buckeyes vending machine, a picture of OSU great A.J. Hawk, and a host of other memorabilia. When Pead's grandpa was a kid, he played with Archie Griffin, the ultimate Ohio State icon who won two Heisman trophies with the Buckeyes in 1974 and 1975. Pead later broke Griffin's career rushing record at Eastmoor Academy in Columbus.

"I would go up to the (Ohio State) facilities as a recruit and watch practices," Pead said. "I spoke with the coaches a lot. Up until a month before signing date, my grades and ACT scores weren't up to their requirements and they said they couldn't give me a scholarship."

Enter Cincinnati running backs coach Tim Hinton. "One of my favorite coaches ever," Pead said.

Cincinnati was also recruiting Pead, who was the state's Division III Player of the Year in 2007, when he ran for 2,204 yards as a senior at Eastmoor with an 11.5-yard average per carry and 39 touchdowns. Nine times out of 10, maybe 10 times out of 10, that recruiting battle would be won by the Buckeyes. But this time the Bearcats had a chance. There was another obstacle, though. West Virginia was interested, too.

Hinton visited Eastmoor and met with each of Pead's teachers to find out what he needed to do to pass each of his classes and qualify for a scholarship. "It was almost like a parent-teacher conference," Pead said.

Pead took it from there.

"Cincinnati never backed out," he said. "(Hinton) had a conversation with me about more than football, about how to be accountable and responsible in life. For a man to have that type of conversation with me, I just respected it. That's what won me over."

Hinton decided to recruit Pead after watching him run in a track meet his junior year. He was impressed by his acceleration and his ability to plant his foot and make an abrupt cut. He feared the competition from West Virginia would be stiff, but he was determined to win because he knew how a dynamic player like Pead would thrive in Kelly's spread offense.

During Pead's recruitment, Hinton also observed how he interacted with a special needs child that his grandparents had adopted and concluded that Pead would be humbled and grounded when he reached college despite his abundant ability.

In fact, Pead was anything but humble when he got to Cincinnati. He knew how good he was and wasn't afraid to express the confidence he had in himself and his teammates. But it took him awhile to reach the point where he could show everyone what he could do.

As a freshman, Pead carried only 30 times for 194 yards, but his average of 6.5 yards per carry was eye-opening. His talent was obvious, especially to Goebel, who feared that Pead might take carries away from both him and Ramsey in 2009.

Goebel suffered a broken hand early in spring practice, then he pulled his hamstring on the first day of fall camp. He remembers vividly that the injury occurred during the 22nd of 24 practice periods. He should have taken himself out, he said, but he thought he was merely cramping.

"I tried to be a tough guy," Goebel said.

He realizes now that there was more to his persistence than just macho football posturing. "Knowing how good Isaiah was, I didn't want him to have a chance to take any reps away from me," Goebel said. "I probably practiced through a few things I shouldn't have, and it probably turned into a few more injuries."

Goebel didn't get his first carry of 2009 until October 24, when he gained 10 yards on six carries against Louisville. In the same game, Pead carried six times for 88 yards and two touchdowns, one coming on a 67-yard run, to give him 280 yards for the season. By then, Goebel wasn't the only one who could see Pead coming on. Ramsey soon discovered that Pead was coming for his reps, too.

"I was just excited to get on the field and make plays," Pead said. "Me and Jacob, we both were from Columbus. We played at rival high schools and had played against each other in high school. For both of us to be in tandem that year, I was excited for it. Throughout training camp, Coach put in a couple of packages that I would be in, and I had an opportunity to make plays. All of us in the running back group, we all wanted to be starters."

Pead scored the first two touchdowns of his college career in the season opener at Rutgers, even though he didn't start that game. His stock continued to rise as the season went on. Goebel carried only 12 times for 41 yards as a senior.

"It was a yin-yang year for me," Goebel said. "It was one of the most exciting teams and situations I've ever been on, but I lost the opportunity to be a future NFL draft pick because I probably was

—

93

a little too excited about my opportunity. It was frustrating, but it was also one of the most amazing experiences ever to go from freshman year where we had people in the stands wearing Ohio State jerseys and there were as many open seats as there were people sitting in them, to where people couldn't get tickets, we're on ESPN, and they're showing people in tents (waiting in line) to get tickets.

"I remember during my freshman year, if you wore something that said 'Cincinnati football,' it was usually because you were on the team or you knew somebody who was on the team and you were wearing their T-shirt. By my senior year, everybody was wearing Bearcat gear and jerseys. It was my first time where I got to experience a little bit of fame. I wasn't even playing that year, but people knew me. I was a running back. I'd go to class and people would ask me football questions. It was an absolutely amazing experience. Going undefeated was outrageously fun."

Pead was just getting started. As a junior, he gained 1,029 yards to become the first Cincinnati running back since Richard Hall in 2004 to gain 1,000 yards in a season. He followed that with 1,259 yards as a senior. During his Cincinnati career, he had nine games of at least 100 yards, including 213 yards against Rutgers on November 20, 2010, the 10th-highest single-game total in school history. He finished his career with 3,288 yards, the third-highest total in school history behind Reggie Taylor (4,242 yards from 1983-86) and DeMarco McCluskey (3,487 yards in 1998 and from 2000-02).

Pead was selected by the St. Louis Rams in the second round of the 2012 draft, the 50th overall pick, but he was unable to duplicate the success he had in college. He played five seasons in the NFL -- four with the Rams and one with the Miami Dolphins -- and gained a total of 100 rushing yards on 27 carries. He also caught 15 passes for 100 yards.

In the early-morning hours of November 12, 2016, he was in a car accident that resulted in the loss of his left leg. Pead has no memory of what occurred that morning. All he knows is what former UC teammate Wesley Richardson, who was in the car with him and escaped with no serious injuries, told him. The Cadillac that Pead was driving on I-670 in Columbus hit a bump in the road. Pead lost control and the car hit a guardrail, which entered the car through the driver's side and pinned his legs behind him. Pead sustained a concussion and blacked out.

Running back Isaiah Pead, who lost his left leg in a 2016 auto accident, rallies the Cincinnati faithful in the 2017 season opener against Austin Peay.

A year later, he was honored on the field before the Bearcats' season opener against Austin Peay at Nippert Stadium.

"That 12-0 season, the firepower we had and the leadership that we had as a team, we were accountable to each other," Pead said. "We faced adversity, persevered through it, and fought through it. Every week when we walked into the Nip, the crowds were getting bigger. When we walked out of the hotel, the crowd was crazy. We're getting on our buses and they're beating on the buses like it's a concert. We're never going to forget that. That came from everyday hard work and being disciplined, with one common goal in mind. We knew that we were walking out of every stadium with a win. You wake up different when all the chips are lined up like that.

"When Kelly left, that's just like something in life that's detrimental and you see things fall apart. The following year we go 4-8 and we were like, 'Whoa, this is not us.' You learn a lot from that. I did, especially me now. I'm at a disadvantage, but I know just because of the man I am and the faith that I have that I will win. I will succeed. That's just personally how I feel about it."

10

Pike Goes Down

When Kelly was asked at Big East Media Day in 2009 what he thought Pike needed to improve on entering his senior season, the Cincinnati coach didn't hesitate.

"Toughness," he said.

Pike had an outstanding season in 2008 after he took over for Grutza, but he missed two games entirely with a broken left forearm that he incurred at Akron and left four others early due to injury.

"We need him to answer the call each and every game," Kelly said. "We played a lot of quarterbacks last year (five to be exact). That made it difficult."

At 6-foot-6, 210 pounds, Pike wasn't a muscular specimen. But when he was asked to respond to Kelly's criticism, he said he had added 15 to 20 pounds of muscle during the offseason and that he was determined to play in every game in 2009.

He had made good on that promise through Cincinnati's first five games, but with No. 21 South Florida (5-0) next on the schedule after a bye week, he was expecting a tough game against a defense that, up to that point in the season, was the best in the league, and a physical one at that.

To add to Pike's concern, Joe Tresey -- who had been

Cincinnati's defensive coordinator during the past two years -- was now in the same role for the Bulls. Tresey knew Pike's strengths and weaknesses from coaching against him every day in practice, and he had the players to make life difficult for the Bearcats' quarterback.

USF was ranked first in the conference in scoring defense (9.4 points per game) and total defense (263.0 yards). Cincinnati was first in scoring offense (42.0) and total offense (468.2 yards). The Bulls had forced 16 turnovers, tied with Rutgers for the most in the league, including seven the previous week in their win over Syracuse.

The USF game marked a return to conference play for the Bearcats, who had played four straight non-league games after knocking off Rutgers in their season opener. At the time, Kelly was looking for more ways to get Gilyard involved in the offense. Gilyard led the Bearcats in catches with 38 and was first in the Big East in scoring with 54 points. Lately, though, teams had started to double-team him.

It was a logical strategy, but it failed to appreciably slow the Bearcats' offense. They simply had too many weapons. Against Miami the week before, Barnett started at wide receiver in place of D.J. Woods and caught six passes for 57 yards. Binns caught five for 83 yards with a 35-yard touchdown against the RedHawks.

"That's when Armon started coming on," Pike said. "As electric as Mardy Gilyard was, toward the end of the season Armon Binns was the go-to on a big play. On third-and-eight, I had to find Armon because Mardy would get so much attention and Armon was so good at beating his defender one-on-one."

The Cincinnati-USF game was played on October 15 before 63,796 fans at Tampa's Raymond James Stadium, also the home of the NFL Tampa Bay Bucs, and was ESPN's featured Thursday night game.

The Bearcats trailed, 7-3, on quarterback B.J. Daniels' 28-yard touchdown pass to Jessie Hester. Pike then connected with Binns on two touchdown passes -- one from three yards, the other from eight -- to give Cincinnati a 17-7 lead. USF's Eric Schwartz kicked a 50-yard field goal with 43 seconds left in the half to pull the Bulls within seven at halftime, 17-10.

Late in the first half, Pike landed hard on his left, non-throwing forearm -- the same one he had broken the year before -- when USF defensive tackle Aaron Harris sacked him for an 11-yard loss at the Cincinnati 21 with a minute and a half remaining. Pike immediately went to the locker room to have his arm examined.

"I knew something wasn't right," he said. "In the locker room there was an X-ray machine that looked like it was from the '80s. The X-rays were just so hard to read. I had a metal plate in my arm (from the surgery he had in 2008). What you couldn't see on the X-ray machine was that the plate had slightly shifted. For me, it was, 'Can I go out there and play without making it worse?' Everyone agreed, 'OK, let's give it a shot.'"

Pike started the second half wearing a black brace on his left forearm unsure of what to expect. Remember, his charge from Kelly during the pre-season was for Pike to be tougher. Well, this time Pike was going to tough it out.

He lasted only one series. On second-and-10 at the USF 17-yard line, Pike was sacked by USF's Craig Marshall for a six-yard loss. His next pass was incomplete. Rogers then missed a 41-yard field goal attempt, keeping the score at 17-10.

When the Bearcats' offense took the field after USF went three-and-out on its first possession of the second half, Collaros was at quarterback. Pike was finished for the night -- and for several weeks to come.

Collaros was one of the five quarterbacks who had been pressed into service in 2008. He threw only four passes that season, completing one for two yards. When he entered the USF game in place of Pike, he had thrown all of 11 passes in 2009, six of which he completed for 129 yards and two touchdowns. One of the touchdowns was a 43-yard strike to Charley Howard during the blowout win over Southeast Missouri State in week two. He hadn't thrown a pass since.

During training camp, with Pike cemented as the starter, Collaros -- from Steubenville, Ohio -- was locked in a competition for the backup spot with fellow redshirt sophomore Chazz Anderson from Pickerington, Ohio. Collaros' reward for prevailing in the competition was to come in against USF to run the Cincinnati offense during a crucial conference road game with the outcome very much in doubt. And he had to do it having thrown only 15 passes in his entire college career.

He had arrived at Cincinnati with glowing high school credentials. He led the Steubenville Big Red to two consecutive

Division III state championships as a junior and senior, going 30-0 as the starting quarterback. In 2006, Collaros was Ohio's D-III Player of the Year after completing 68 percent of his passes for 2,550 yards and 30 touchdowns with only four interceptions. He also rushed for 720 yards and 15 TDs. The only thing that prevented him from being a more sought-after recruit was his lack of height. He stood only six feet tall and weighed 209 pounds.

As he trotted onto the field to face USF's stingy defense, the usually confident Collaros was admittedly nervous.

"My buddy Jason (Kelce) hugged me and said, 'You're going to be all right,'" Collaros said. The other players on offense all chimed in, telling him, "You're going to get us through this."

On his first play, Collaros handed the ball to Pead, who was stopped for a one-yard loss. Collaros kept the ball on the next play and was stopped for no gain. Facing third-and-11 at their own 25, still leading by only seven points, the Bearcats called timeout. The next play was a quarterback draw, a play designed to set up Rogers to punt the ball back to USF in an attempt to flip field position.

Collaros stunned everyone by running 75 yards for a touchdown with 8:34 left in the third quarter, giving Cincinnati a 24-10 lead.

"It was a pretty obvious call for a redshirt sophomore," Collaros said. "I took the snap, I think (center Chris) Jurek and Kelce got a good push on the nose guard. Jacob Ramsey really led the way through there. Guys blocked downfield. Their safety took a bad angle on me and I found some room to run.

"Usually when you get a call like that you're trying to negate the damage that could be done. You're not risking anything with the ball being in the air. It's really on me just to not fumble. It was just a really well-executed play."

To make it even sweeter, the touchdown run had come against a USF defense being overseen by Tresey, who had recruited Collaros for Cincinnati out of high school.

"All of my closest friends on the team were going nuts," Collaros said. "I remember Craig Carey running out, jumping on me and hugging me. I remember Kelly saying we still have two quarters left or something like that. It was a really interesting night. I still had a flip phone because I never wanted to succumb to the iPhone. I think my phone was dead. When I got back to Cincinnati, I think I had 300 text messages."

Pike watched Collaros' run while standing on the sideline icing his forearm.

The touchdown run was a huge psychological lift for the Bearcats and their fans. Collaros had wasted no time letting everyone know that everything would be OK even without Pike's commanding presence under center.

Kelly's philosophy when it came to injuries was simple: "Next man in." Those three words were meant to signify that there was no need to panic because of an injury. In this case, it was easy for Pike's teammates to fully embrace that philosophy because they had seen Collaros in practice and they knew what he could do.

"I knew that Zach possessed one thing that Tony didn't have

-- his legs," Gilyard said. "Zach was just short. When Zach rolls out and throws, he has a beautiful ball. I knew we had a good backup. I knew we were good."

The Bearcats went on to beat USF, 34-17, improving their record to 6-0. Collaros finished with 132 rushing yards on 10 carries, with two touchdowns. He threw only seven passes, completing four for 72 yards without a touchdown pass or an interception.

Cincinnati officials said after the game that Pike's injury was a sprained left wrist, but it was much more serious that that. Pike was pleased to see how well Collaros had played in his absence because it meant his team was in good hands. But in the back of his mind he wondered what the injury would mean for him personally.

"You're a Top 10 team in the country," Pike said, "and you're undefeated and you're on this collision path to go wherever you can go. As a senior personally, that was a hard hit to take. At the time you don't know. Am I going to be out for the rest of the year? Is this going to affect me in the NFL? Where does my career go from here? It was a tough week."

The following week the first BCS computer rankings came out and 6-0 Cincinnati was ranked No. 5. These were the rankings that counted, the ones that would determine which two teams would play for the national championship, and the undefeated Bearcats were solidly in the mix. The top five teams were Florida, Alabama, Texas, Boise State and Cincinnati.

Under the BCS system, which was in place from 1998 through 2013, only the top two teams in the rankings qualified for the playoffs that determine the national champion, unlike the College Football Playoff format, which was instituted in 2014. Under that system, the top four teams qualify.

Ever the politician, Kelly immediately began to campaign for his team as a national championship contender, knowing full well there were people in the media inclined to dismiss what the Bearcats were doing.

"There's a system set up," Kelly said. "But you have these people that say it doesn't matter, Cincinnati is not playing for the national championship. That's a bunch of baloney. If you keep winning, keep playing and doing the right things, every team should have a fair opportunity at it. Let the teams play. The rankings are what they are. Let it play itself out. We continue to go down the same road. Are they worthy or not?"

11

Collaros' First Start

If there was one thing Collaros had learned during his first two years in college, it was that the 30-0 record the Steubenville Big Red had compiled with him starting at quarterback meant nothing at this level. As training camp began in 2009, he was No. 3 on the depth chart behind Pike and Anderson. Just as Pike had his revelation with Kelly the year before, Collaros was about to have his. The difference was that in this case it was Collaros who initiated the conversation.

When he asked Kelly what he had to do to get more playing time, the Cincinnati coach, in his distinctly blunt manner, told Collaros he didn't like the way he practiced. He also told his young quarterback that he shouldn't try to make a big play every time the ball was snapped. There were times when he needed to appreciate the value of a short or intermediate pass, or even an incompletion. And even though he didn't want to completely discourage Collaros from improvising -- after all, that was one of his strengths -- he preferred for him to operate mostly within the confines of the offense he had so painstakingly developed over the years. Collaros got the message.

As the week leading up to October 24 Louisville game

unfolded, Kelly did his best to keep alive the possibility -- at least in the minds of the Cardinals' coaching staff -- that Pike might start after all. Pike underwent surgery on Tuesday to repair the plate that had been inserted into his left forearm in 2008 after he broke the arm against Akron, the one that had shifted after he absorbed two punishing hits in the South Florida game.

But reporters were told that Pike participated in Monday's light workout and was examined after practice by team orthopedist Dr. Angelo Colosimo. At that point, so the story went, the determination was made to hold Pike out of practice for two days to see how his arm responded. After that, Pike would try to practice to see if he could play against Louisville.

That's what Kelly wanted Louisville to believe. In fact, the surgery had already been performed and Collaros was told Wednesday that he would be the starter against Louisville on Saturday. He took most of the snaps in practice and immersed himself in preparation for his first career start.

It fell to Kelly, offensive coordinator Jeff Quinn, passing game coordinator Charley Molnar, and quarterbacks coach Greg Forest to adjust the offense to fit Collaros' strengths. The adjustment wasn't nearly as difficult as it could have been because Collaros played with a style similar to that of Dustin Grutza, Pike's predecessor, with his running ability as a major part of his arsenal.

"We were already pivoting back to what we had started with," Kelly said, "so we were OK with it. We were ready to go right away."

Pike's role that week was two-fold: to help Collaros prepare for the game and to work to minimize his down time. It helped that Pike and his teammates had so much confidence in Collaros.

"Zach just had a whole different ability level," Pike said. "He didn't have the height advantage, but he was a tough kid from Steubenville, Ohio. He was going to do whatever it takes to win, whether it's with his arms or his legs or running somebody over for a first down. You just knew you were in good hands with Zach. That helped me in so many ways while I was rehabbing, being able to say, 'OK, we can still do this. I can get back and still make a run at this and we can still be undefeated.' Having Zach in that spot was very comforting."

Pike and Collaros had enjoyed a good relationship long before Pike was injured. Based on what he had accomplished the year before, Pike was the unchallenged starter going into the season, so there was no sense of competition between them. Collaros, a sophomore with two more years to play, understood that Pike would run the show this year, opening the door for him to take over in 2010, providing he could beat out Anderson again.

But there was more to their relationship than Collaros merely accepting the established pecking order. He genuinely liked being around Pike, whom he calls "one of the funniest guys I know."

When Collaros first got to Cincinnati in 2007, Pike was still buried on the depth chart. Kelly hadn't yet had his heart-to-heart chat with Pike, so he wasn't infused with the sense of urgency that served him and the Bearcats so well in 2008 and 2009.

"It was my third day (at Cincinnati)," Collaros said. "We were working out and somebody said, 'You've got to meet this guy, the quarterback.' We worked out together and Tony was maybe the biggest smack-off ever. I belly laughed. I cried during the whole workout. I got nothing done. After a while, you kind of get accustomed to his humor, but I remember that first time meeting him I was laughing my ass off."

The Battle for the Victory Bell against Miami was the Bearcats' longest-running rivalry, but the Battle for the Keg of Nails against Louisville probably meant more to the players. Unlike Miami, which was in the same conference as the Bearcats for only a brief time -- from 1947 to 1952 in the Mid-American Conference -- Cincinnati and Louisville played against each other in the Missouri Valley Conference from 1957 through 1969; in Conference USA from 1996 to 2004; and now in the Big East beginning in 2005. The two schools, located about 100 miles from each other, also played each other as independents every year from 1970 until 1992. Entering the 2009 season, the Bearcats held a 27-21-1 advantage over the Cardinals in a series that started in 1922. But the Cardinals had won five of the previous six.

After the win over USF, the Bearcats had risen to fifth in the AP poll with a 6-0 overall record, 2-0 in the Big East. Louisville was 2-4 overall, 0-2 in the league, and ranked last in scoring offense with 21.8 points per game, just a little over half of what Cincinnati was averaging.

A crowd of 35,099 showed up on a cold, windy, late Saturday

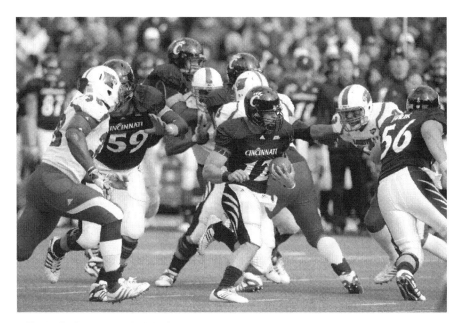

Zach Collaros made his first career start against Louisville and passed for 253 yards with three touchdowns in the Bearcats' 41-10 victory.

afternoon at Nippert Stadium to watch Collaros' debut as a starter, eager to find out if what he did against USF was the result of adrenalin or if the Bearcats' quarterback of the future was capable of keeping them unbeaten until Pike returned.

Long before kickoff, Collaros was sitting on a bench outside the locker room at the north end of the stadium contemplating his first collegiate start when Kelly approached him. The conversation had nothing to do with game strategy.

"He said, 'Hey, uh, you know this game's on ESPN (actually ESPNU),'" Collaros said. "I'm already nervous. I said, 'Yeah, Coach, I know.' I was just thinking, be cool, calm and collected, telling myself, 'You've got this.' Then he looks at me and he says, 'If I yell at you, if you yell back at me, you're coming out of the game.'

"Right, wrong or whatever, I always have an opinion, and there were a couple of times in practice where we would disagree and he would tell me, 'I'm going to give you a black jersey and put you on defense.' That's one of the clearest memories I have of my entire time as a player. That interaction with BK was so funny to me. It kind of calmed me down. He gave me a little wink and laughed. At the time, I was deathly afraid."

Collaros needn't have worried because Kelly scripted the first 15 plays for him, and as Collaros would quickly discover, "He was a master of the first 15 plays."

Kelly told him to get the ball to Gilyard early, knowing that once Gilyard got involved, the offense would start rolling. The first play was a run for Gilyard, who gained five yards. He also caught one pass for 16 yards and a first down. The Bearcats needed only 10 plays to go 78 yards for their first touchdown, on Pead's one-yard run to take a 7-0 lead with 10:10 left in the first quarter. After the Cardinals went three-and-out on their first possession, Cincinnati charged down the field again, this time going 90 yards in nine plays, covering two minutes, 49 seconds, scoring on Collaros' 24-yard touchdown pass to Binns. It had taken only 19 plays from scrimmage – four more than Kelly had scripted -- for the Bearcats to take a 14-0 lead.

Cincinnati led, 21-7, at the half and 38-10 after three quarters. The Bearcats walked off the field with a 41-10 victory and possession of the Keg of Nails. They had won their seventh game of the season without a loss for the first time since 1954 when coach Sid

Gillman, an offensive innovator in his own right who was a member of the Pro Football and College Football Hall of Fame, was in

charge. That team finished 8-2.

Collaros played a nearly perfect game against Louisville with 15 completions in 17 pass attempts for 253 yards and three touchdowns without a sack. He also ran 11 times for 52 yards. Pead carried six times for 88 yards and two touchdowns. Gilyard, Binns and Woods each had more than 50 receiving yards.

Brian Kelly told Collaros to get Mardy Gilyard involved early in the game against Louisville.

"I was hoping Tony Pike would play," Louisville coach Steve Kragthorpe said after the game. "It makes them one-dimensional and a better matchup for us. I knew Collaros could run."

Collaros had gone about things a little differently from Pike, but the Cincinnati offense was still hitting on all cylinders.

"You never know until somebody gets into a game and starts playing, but Zach was a really confident individual, very smart, very competitive," Kelce said. "We knew, if given the opportunity, he would get the job done. His coming-out party at South Florida had been maybe a little bit more than any of us were expecting, especially as good as South Florida was that year, and it being an away game. That was a big stage for him to showcase what kind of player he was."

It was a difficult time for Pike, who was worried about what the future held for him while trying to be a good teammate to his replacement. He was relieved to hear that his surgery had been successful. It turned out that the metal plate in his arm had not shifted. What really happened, according to Mangine, is that the bone started to buckle on the plate when Pike absorbed the hit at South Florida.

"(Colosimo) put another plate in there, got it straightened and then he played," Mangine said. "We just had to take that one out and refresh the plate."

Once the procedure was finished and Pike was assured that he would be OK, the psychological burden he was carrying was eased.

"I knew at the time that whatever was going in there was going to be steady and hold," Pike said. "Having the assurance of the doctor saying that you can play again this year, to go from the emotions of 'OK, I'm in the Heisman race, to now my season and probably my career is over too,' to 'You're going to get back this year,' changed the whole dynamic of fighting to get back quicker."

Spotlight

Mitch's Mission

Mitch Stone was 11 years old in February 2009, a fifth-grader and straight A student at Maddux Elementary School in the suburban Forest Hills School District, when he started to have headaches and getting sick for no apparent reason. After he returned home from school one afternoon, his mother noticed that his right eye looked different. It seemed to be turned inward.

"I couldn't control it," Mitch said. "I didn't know it was happening, so we called the doctor. That's when they found the (brain) tumor. Three days later I underwent surgery."

In July, Mitch and his family were approached by the Cincinnati football team about being "adopted" by the Bearcats under the auspices of the Friends of Jaclyn Foundation.

At first Mitch was reluctant to get involved. He didn't like the way he looked and didn't want a lot of attention while going through such a trying time. But his family, especially his identical twin brother, Nick, talked him into it.

"They said this would be an amazing opportunity," Mitch said. "I was a big Bearcat fan, but I had a lot going on at the time. Nick was like, 'Man, you've got to do this. This can be so cool. Just think, we'll get to hang out with the players and go on the field.'"

Mitch's radiologist first reached out to him with the adoption idea, but it originated with Ernest Jones, the Bearcats' director of player services. Jones had heard about the Friends of Jaclyn Foundation, which is dedicated to improving the quality of life for children diagnosed with brain tumors by matching the child with a college or high school sports team. When he consulted with doctors and nurses at Cincinnati Children's Hospital, they suggested Mitch.

Jones presented the idea to Kelly, who was all for it. His players also were overwhelmingly in favor of it. They met Mitch in July and put together an adoption "ceremony" to make it official. The Bearcats thus became the first college football team in the country to become involved in the program. Mitch's Mission was born. Everyone in the Cincinnati football program, from the coaches on down, wore a red, white and blue bracelet with the words "Mitch's Mission" written on it.

"It was amazing," Stone said. "I went to campus after a summer practice and they took me and my family into the team room. They did an introduction and told me we're happy to have you on our team. They were kind of swarming in around me and they gave me a lot of swag, a lot of cool stuff that Nick could wear too. It was really a good way for me to get my mind off the constant treatment that I was going through at the time. I went to a few practices during the summer, but that was during the period when I was receiving chemotherapy, so that made it very difficult to go to a lot of practices.

"During the fall, I was still undergoing the chemotherapy. I would be in the hospital for three weeks receiving treatment and then they would let me out for a week. I went to a game during that time and I got to go up to one of the coaches' boxes and sat with them and their families, and my family was allowed to join us. I got to watch a lot of games. That was really special, being a fan of Bearcat football my entire life."

It was even more special because the Bearcats kept winning week after week. By the end of the season, they had put together the best season in Cincinnati football history, and Mitch was a big part of it. He was allowed to go into the locker room before the games, just before the Bearcats took the field. He marveled at the surroundings and at how emotionally fired up the Bearcats were.

Because of his low white blood cell count, there were times when Mitch wasn't allowed to see many people, so the Cincinnati players chipped in $5 apiece to buy him a pre-paid cell phone with a monthly plan so he could stay in touch with them. If he was having a bad day, Mitch could call a player. And they could call and text him.

Gilyard would call periodically just to shoot the breeze and ask how school was going. Ricardo Mathews called and sang Happy Birthday over the phone. Mitch appreciated every call, every text, but he grew especially close to Goebel.

They would pray together before games and became friends. Several years later Goebel invited Mitch and his family to his wedding.

"When Mitch and his family came, that was right in line with everything the guys were about," Goebel said. "We gave him a

Travis Kelce and the Bearcats adopted 11-year-old Mitch Stone and made him an important part of the 2009 team.

standing ovation. A lot of our guys, we could relate. It was a lot of guys who weren't getting everything on a silver platter. They weren't getting scholarships to Ohio State. They had to earn everything they had.

"We knew right away there was something different about this kid. I felt like he was going to be getting a lot of love from a lot of people, but I wanted to reach out to him and talk to him on a regular person level and get to know his family a little bit. I just wanted him to be able to see that and see that it's not all Saturday with the lights on and wearing the uniform. Ninety-eight percent of it is a grind and having to work your butt off."

Goebel was going through a difficult time of his own, missing a big chunk of the season with his hamstring injury. Seeing what Mitch was going through provided him with badly needed perspective.

"Seeing him show up for games in the shape that he was in and knowing what he was going through, we were like, 'It's not too bad,'" Goebel said. "'I don't have it too bad with my injuries.' Yeah, it was very frustrating, but I was like, 'Dude, you're alive. You're getting your education paid for. It could be a lot worse and if this kid can do what he's doing, then you can do what you're doing.'

"There were times when he couldn't show up because he wasn't healthy enough and it would be bad for him to be in front of everybody. It kind of weighs on you heavy. It helped us grow together as a team. It gave us this kindred spirit of it didn't matter what your beliefs were or where you were from. Everybody was rooting for him. We all wanted what was best for him."

By the time the Sugar Bowl rolled around, Mitch had built up enough immunity that his doctors allowed him to go to the game. He remembers it was around Halloween when he was told that he was in remission and that it was just a matter of time before the tumor would be gone. The Friends of Jaclyn Foundation paid for him and his family to travel to New Orleans, and he was allowed to attend practices leading up the game.

Mitch is healthy now and is a business student at Cincinnati. He volunteers to serve on the Patient Advisory Council at Children's Hospital. The Mitch's Mission Foundation sponsors an annual Play

Date with the Bearcats.

"We thought, 'How can we give back to all the people who helped us get through this experience'?" Mitch said. "We knew we wanted to help kids. Mitch's Mission is a non-profit that raises money to send kids with cancer to summer camp every year."

The decision to invite Mitch and his family to his wedding, Goebel said, grew out of a desire by him and his fiancé to be around people who had molded them into who they were as they embarked on their life together.

"I felt like he gave me some spirit that helped me become the man that my wife was marrying and gave me perspective, their whole family," Goebel said. "I wanted them to be able to see this. You think of college football, and you hear stories about guys that are crazy or partying or are womanizers. That's not everybody. I wanted Mitch to see that this is cool, too. You can do this and still be one of the guys with everyone. We both wanted them there because they put smiles on our faces and made us feel loved."

So much happened during the 2009 season that was memorable, but nothing was more heartwarming than the story of the Bearcats' relationship with Mitch Stone and his family.

"They gave me a lot of support that I needed at the time," Mitch said. "I was like, 'The football team's got our back. There's a way to get through this.'"

When I mentioned to Kelly that Mitch was healthy and a student at Cincinnati, the Notre Dame coach's face lit up, as if he had just witnessed a Pike-to-Gilyard touchdown pass.

"That's fabulous," Kelly said. "It was kind of an interesting time for us. Our guys were so focused on themselves and how they could get better. Mitch gave us an opportunity as a team to think about others. He just became so important to the identity of our football team. It was one of those things that we needed to strengthen our football team. Our guys just embraced him like nothing I've seen before on any football team that I've had. And it was genuine and authentic. We both benefited from that relationship.

"He had a horrific disease at that age. You don't know if you're going to make it. That group was such a tough-minded group. They were hardscrabble. To have somebody else that they could rally around, kind of like, 'That's our guy.' It created a real strong dynamic."

12

Collaros in Charge

Under Collaros, the offense that Pike had run so efficiently was functioning as smoothly as ever. It had been only two games, but Collaros was playing as if he had been the starter all season, plus he added a new dimension with his running ability. Cincinnati fans weren't saying, "Tony, who?" just yet, but some were beginning to question whether Collaros should remain the starter after Pike returned.

Collaros did nothing to change their minds, given the way he played against Syracuse on October 31 before 33,802 fans at the Carrier Dome. The Orange, who were in their first season under head coach Doug Marrone, were 3-4 overall, 0-2 in the league, seemingly not the kind of opponent to threaten the Bearcats' perfect season. But when Kelly watched the game film, he saw how hard Syracuse was playing under Marrone and worried that the Orange could cause problems for his team. He took pains all week to warn his players not to take this game for granted.

The Bearcats prevailed, 28-7, to go 8-0 overall, 4-0 in the Big East. Collaros turned in another outstanding performance, completing 22 of 28 passes for 295 yards with four touchdown passes and no interceptions. But a lot of what he did statistically in this

121

game was not the result of his capable steering of Kelly's offense. It was based on his ability to improvise, the very thing that Kelly had asked him to rein in before the season started.

The first time Collaros pulled a rabbit out of his hat occurred midway through the first quarter. On third-and-11 from the Cincinnati 19, he was chased out of the pocket and looked to be in trouble when he flipped the ball to Binns, who was all alone a few yards downfield. Binns sprinted down the sideline for an 81-yard touchdown.

Collaros was forced to get creative again after Syracuse came right back with a 75-yard touchdown drive to tie the score at 7-7. This time he was the holder on a 33-yard field goal attempt by Rogers. But the field goal was never attempted. The snap from Mike Windt was a little low, although entirely manageable. Still, Collaros didn't handle it very well, so he grabbed the ball and rolled out looking for someone to throw to, finding tight end Kazeem Alli in the end zone for another touchdown to make it 14-7.

Living up to Kelly's concerns, the Orange threatened to tie the game before halftime when they advanced to the Cincinnati eight-yard line, only to have Frey intercept quarterback Greg Paulus' pass.

On the Bearcats' first possession of the second half, Collaros improvised again on a 13-yard touchdown pass to Binns. Again, he was forced to scramble. With nowhere to go, and fearing that the play was about to break down, he lofted the ball high in the air, hoping that Binns would be able to out-jump his defender, which he did, to put Cincinnati ahead, 21-7.

Late in the third quarter, with Syracuse driving deep into Cincinnati territory, the defense came up big again when Derek Wolfe hit Orange running back Delone Carter to force a fumble at the Cincinnati seven-yard line. Wolfe recovered the fumble himself.

Binns had a monster game with five catches for 138 yards and two touchdowns. Gilyard caught six passes for 62 yards, and Pead ran 16 times for 77 yards. The Bearcats gained 422 yards to 283 for Syracuse.

When the game was over, Kelly breathed a sigh of relief.

"That was the one as a coach that I was worried about," he said.

Maybe he should have been a little more concerned about the next game against Connecticut, which turned out to be a wild, high-scoring affair in which the Bearcats broke the school record for total offense in a game.

The Huskies, coached by Randy Edsall, were hurting emotionally as they prepared to face the Bearcats. Several weeks earlier, on October 18, Connecticut cornerback Jasper Howard was stabbed to death, sending a shock through the program. After Howard's death, the Bearcats sent a banner signed by Kelly and the entire team and staff to the Huskies featuring a blue C-paw with Howard's picture and the phrase, "Teammates for Life." Now the Bearcats were faced with the task of trying to beat the team they had reached out to console just a few weeks earlier.

By then, Kelly had become one of the hottest -- if not the

hottest -- coaching names in the country. Already during his tenure at Cincinnati, he had been mentioned as a candidate to fill vacancies at Tennessee and Michigan. I asked Kelly after he had been connected to Michigan in 2007 if that was a job he might be interested in. He told me there are only two jobs he would leave Cincinnati for: Notre Dame and an NFL head-coaching job. He had no interest in being an NFL coordinator.

Now, even though there were still four games to go in Kelly's third season at Cincinnati, every college football fan in the country knew that Weis was on the hot seat at Notre Dame, and that Kelly was already being mentioned in the media as leading candidate to replace him.

With that in mind, I talked to Kelly leading up to the Connecticut game about whether he really planned to be at Cincinnati for the long haul. He talked about the talent he had in the program and the commitment the university was making to football. In addition to the new practice facility that was already in the works, he wanted Nippert Stadium renovated and the seating capacity increased to 45,000.

"This can't be as good as it gets," Kelly said. "And they know that. Our president (Greg Williams) knows that. He's made that clear to me. Within five years, we want this stadium completed."

Eventually, he said, Cincinnati could stack up against 90 percent of the college football programs in the country. "There's got to be just a small sliver of schools out there that would have more than Cincinnati."

A few days later, with ABC's top broadcasting team of Brent Musburger, Kirk Herbstreit and Lisa Salters on hand at Nippert to call the game, the Bearcats -- ranked fourth in the AP poll -- put up 711 yards of total offense before a sellout crowd of 35,100. The way the game unfolded, they needed every one of those yards to get past UConn.

At the time, Cincinnati had the top-ranked defense in the conference, allowing 313.2 yards per game, and the seventh-ranked scoring defense in the country, allowing 13.7 points per game, to go with the top-ranked offense, which was churning out 454 yards per game. The Bearcats were one of seven unbeaten teams in the country, along with Alabama, Texas, Boise State, Iowa, Florida and Texas Christian. They were No. 5 in the BCS standings.

UConn's 4-4 record (1-3 in the Big East) was underwhelming, but the Huskies had been ahead in the fourth quarter in each of their four losses. Starting quarterback Cody Endres had suffered a shoulder injury in the first quarter of the Huskies' loss to Rutgers the previous week and was expected to be finished for the season. But his backup, Zach Frazer, had come off the bench to pass for a career-high 333 yards.

"I remember that whole week getting to meet Brent Musburger and Kirk Herbstreit," Collaros said. "The energy at Nippert Stadium, especially Nippert at night, it was hard to express how amazing it was to play in there. That night it was especially electric. We got the ball early to Mardy Gilyard and got him going. I know Jake Ramsey busted a big run. Isaiah had an unbelievable

125

night. A lot of the plays in that game were handoffs to Isaiah. A lot of the cuts he was making, were like, 'Oh my God, what a cut.'"

Ramsey carried 12 times for 91 yards in the Bearcats' 47-45 win. Pead gained 67 yards on 10 carries and scored two touchdowns. Gilyard caught 12 passes for 172 yards, and Binns caught five passes for 108 yards and one touchdown.

Those were all impressive performances, but Collaros turned in the most dazzling, with 480 passing yards and 75 rushing yards. He passed for one touchdown and ran for two. His 480 yards were the second-highest total in school history behind Greg Cook's 554 yards against Ohio in 1968. Collaros completed 29 of his 37 passes.

"You just felt like every throw you made was going to be caught," Collaros said. "It was one of those kind of nights."

In a game filled with big offensive plays, the one that stands out for Kelly was a pass that Collaros heaved out of bounds just before the end of the first half. Cincinnati had started its final drive of the half on its own 38-yard line with 21 seconds left. On the first play of the drive, Collaros connected with sophomore tight end Adrien Robinson for 54 yards down the sideline, setting up the Bearcats at the UConn eight. After an incomplete pass intended for Woods, the Bearcats lined up on second-and-goal to kick a field goal, but the snap was low and Collaros had trouble handling it. Instead of losing yardage and letting time expire, he rolled out and threw out of bounds to stop the clock.

"Every coach lies through their ass and says, 'We rehearse that all the time,'" Kelly said. "We rehearsed it maybe three times in camp and we went over it after that maybe once or twice. Most kids would not have done what he did. He was just on it because there only a few seconds left. It hit me right there that our kids were really locked in offensively."

Collaros was called for intentional grounding, which pushed the Bearcats back to the UConn 17. But his quick thinking gave Rogers the chance to kick one of his four field goals as time ran out to give Cincinnati a 30-10 halftime lead. At that point, the Bearcats had already gained 457 yards.

UConn's Jordan Todman, who rushed for 162 yards, ran for a 46-yard touchdown to make it 30-17 five minutes into the second half. Collaros needed only two minutes, 50 seconds to move Cincinnati 80 yards for a touchdown, which he scored himself on a 28-yard run to put the Bearcats ahead 37-17. UConn's Robert McClain returned a Rogers punt 87 yards for a touchdown and it was 37-24 at the end of the third quarter.

A 35-yard field goal by Rogers improved Cincinnati's lead to 16 at 40-24. The Huskies then drove 68 yards in five plays and scored on Todman's one-yard run to cut the deficit to 40-32. Todman scored again on a two-yard run and UConn went for two in an attempt to tie the score. But Frazer's pass was incomplete, leaving the Bearcats clinging to a 40-38 lead.

Gilyard returned the kickoff 43 yards to the Cincinnati 44. Eight plays later, Pead ran 14 yards for a touchdown. Rogers' extra point kick gave the Bearcats a seemingly safe 47-38 lead with 1:52 remaining, but the Huskies scored again on Frazer's nine-yard touchdown pass with 13 seconds left. Dave Teggart's extra point kick made it 47-45.

UConn still had a chance if it could recover an onside kick, but Cincinnati's Charley Howard fell on the ball at the Huskies' 41, which enabled Collaros to take a knee to run out the clock.

"That game was done and over with," Kelly said. "They couldn't stop us. We were rolling up and down the field. They had no answers for us. They had some issues at safety and we were taking advantage of them left and right. And then all of a sudden the dam broke defensively for us."

UConn finished with 462 yards of total offense -- 261 passing and 201 rushing -- against what to that point was the Big East's top-ranked defense. After that game, the Cincinnati defense slipped to fourth in the Big East.

"It was an opposite preparation," Diaco said. "It wasn't how we practiced every day. It wasn't how our team was built. It wasn't like playing against the triple option, but close. And they were handing the ball to a dynamic back. They were a damn good football team."

Collaros had put together one of the greatest games of any quarterback in Cincinnati history, but he, too, has a memory from that game more personal than the numbers he put up, a memory that provides insight into his playful personality and his evolving relationship with Kelly.

"I changed a play call for the first time in that game," Collaros said. "It was fourth-and-two. I think we called a timeout. We had two tight ends on the backside and we were going to move the pocket to the left. I remember looking at the matchup and D.J. Woods had man coverage. It was supposed to be a go on the outside, a five-yard out by D.J.

"I wasn't great at rolling out and throwing that little out. I was better at throwing to the corner, so I changed the play call. D.J. did a great job of getting the guy turned around. I babied the throw, but he made a good catch. I remember running by the sideline and Kelly was looking at me like he was saying, 'You little gunslinger,' or some shit like that. Once I got to know (Kelly) I think our personalities meshed pretty well together. I'm a pretty serious guy, but I like to have fun too. I think he's the same way."

Collaros also remembers coming off the field after failing to get a first down when Kelly called a quarterback run on third-and-four.

"We had 42 points and we were getting booed," he said. "That was pretty funny."

The Bearcats' continued offensive success, even without Pike, was a tribute to Collaros, but also to his teammates on offense, including a stout offensive line that made it all go. And it was a statement about the effectiveness of Kelly's offense and his ability to tailor it to his personnel.

"The system was innovative," Kelce said. "It was new. It was forward thinking. We had all the pieces to make it successful. We had a great offensive line with Jeff Linkenbach, who played in the

NFL for a long time. We had Alex Hoffman, who was a really good player. Sam Griffin played really well for us."

Center Chris Jurek was a first-team all-Big East selection. Kelce and Linkenbach were both named to the second team. Take that line, add two outstanding quarterbacks in Pike and Collaros, along with Gilyard, Binns, Woods, Guidugli and others, and the Bearcats' offense was loaded. It was also brimming with confidence.

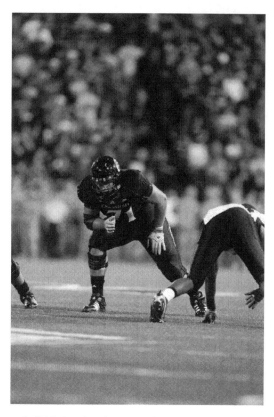

Jeff Linkenbach was a key component in the Bearcats' formidable offensive line.

"Any time we didn't score we were upset," Kelce said. "Even when we were playing Florida in the Sugar Bowl, we felt like we could have put up more points. We were really a confident group, to say the least. Even when we were down against Pittsburgh we knew that if we could get things rolling offensively, if we could give Tony some time and let him throw the ball, we were going to get something going."

Kelce was another on a long list of players who led the

Bearcats to the brink of the national championship game without having the pedigree that usually accompanies such high-caliber teams. The Cleveland Heights, Ohio, native started his Cincinnati career as a walk-on linebacker. When Kelly and his right-hand man, Longo, took over they looked at Kelce and saw an offensive lineman.

He had been moved as an experiment during spring practice in 2007 and did so well that Kelly told him he wanted to keep him on the offensive line. Kelce was willing to do the work in the weight room that he'd need for his new position, but in exchange he wanted a scholarship. Kelly agreed.

This was a program that put up 15 straight regular season wins tp that point without elite-ranked talent. In 2006, Cincinnati's recruiting class was ranked 102nd by Rivals, 80th by Scout. Cincinnati's 2007 recruiting was ranked 89th by Scout, 80th by Rivals. The 2008 and 2009 classes were afforded a little more respect, but still didn't come in higher than the 50s or 60s.

It's no wonder the Bearcats took great pride in what they were able to accomplish with players that, for the most part, weren't highly regarded coming out of high school.

Collaros was considered too short. Pike had only two scholarship offers. Demetrius Jones wasn't good enough to play at Notre Dame. Kelce was a walk-on. Ohio State didn't want Pead. And on special teams, Rogers was pressed into service as a punter when freshman Patrick O'Donnell, now the punter for the Chicago Bears, went out with an injury three games into the season.

In addition to leading the Bearcats in scoring with 102 points

(13 of 19 field goals plus 63 of 65 extra points), Rogers averaged 41.6 yards per punt while filling the unenviable role of replacing first-team All-American punter Kevin Huber.

"Those were big shoes to fill," Rogers said, "and I knew I wouldn't fill them. I was confident that I could punt, but I'm not Kevin Huber on the punting side. It was more about making solid connection with the ball and trying to place it on the side that was called to give our team a chance to get down there and make a play."

Kelly focused his recruiting within a three-hour radius of Cincinnati. His goal was to build his program around the ideal Bearcats player, which to him, was a player who was overlooked, "but had a passion that was bigger than the 5-star. We capitalized on that, no doubt."

Another of those diamonds in the rough was Gilyard, who began his college career as a defensive back under Dantonio, then was forced to sit out a year for academic reasons. When Kelly took over, he switched Gilyard to wide receiver, where he became an immediate sensation. In addition to his 172 receiving yards against UConn, he totaled 144 yards in kickoff return yardage for 303 yards of all-purpose offense. It was another remarkable performance for the team's most colorful player, a player whose life story endeared him to Cincinnati fans almost as much as his on-field accomplishments.

13

Mardy on Tuesday or Mardy on Saturday?

After a season away from the program, Gilyard returned for his first game on Thursday, August 30 in the 2007 season opener against Southeast Missouri State.

Before the game, his eyes clouded over with tears when he saw his name on the back of his jersey, and he thought about what he had been through to get back on the field after losing his scholarship for academic reasons in 2006. In his first game back, he caught eight passes for 134 yards, including a 56-yard touchdown reception.

A few days later, I interviewed Gilyard for the first time as we sat at the bottom of the concrete stairs that led from the north end of Nippert Stadium up to the Bearcats' locker room. That's when he told me he had to work four different jobs to pay his tuition before he got his scholarship back, that he had been forced to sleep in his car for several weeks in June while the car was parked overnight behind the CVS store near campus. When he went to sleep at night, he hoped he would wake up in the morning undisturbed so he could begin another grueling workday.

In his early teens, he was already on the streets selling drugs in Bunnell, Florida, he said, and was once shot by someone in a passing car. Getting a chance to play college football at Cincinnati helped

Mardy Gilyard's outsize personality was almost as important to the Bearcats' 2009 success as his play on the field.

him escape all that, and he had almost blown it. But he was smart enough to understand that for his own good he couldn't go home during the year he was forced to sit out. When he returned to football, he was determined to make the most of his second chance.

Gilyard was the most colorful player on a Cincinnati team loaded with personalities. He had a dynamic, fun-loving personality to go with his abundant talent, and was everybody's friend on the team. If there was one person who personified the Bearcats' offensive brilliance, it was Gilyard.

"On the field, you knew what Mardy was," Pike said, "and that was an electric playmaker. I knew that my job was to get Mardy as many touches as possible because you know if Mardy gets enough touches something special is going to happen. If there were two or three series where I wasn't getting him the ball, then I had to figure out a way to do it."

Gilyard did things his way. Sometimes that meant not practicing early in the week when he thought his body needed a break from all the contact he absorbed as the Bearcats' best receiver, kickoff returner and punt returner.

"Do you want Mardy on Tuesday, or do you want Mardy on Saturday?" Gilyard would ask the coaching staff.

"I had no problem with it," Pike said. "There were times when Mardy was hurt and people wanted him to go, but he couldn't. It's a violent game, and we were asking him to do a lot. "

Gilyard said he asked to be excused from practice only once.

"I was just tired one day," he said. "I just said, 'I'm not with it today, Coach. My body hurts.' He didn't want to give me a bone. I'm not going to take the whole day off. It was just something I didn't feel like doing. It was just a couple of drills. I just didn't want to do them. My body was hurting."

Others say it was a frequent occurrence and even became a running joke among staff members. Kelly became accustomed to it. He didn't like it, but he understood and tried to get Gilyard to see his side of the story, which was that ultimately it would benefit Gilyard to practice every day, even if he wasn't always at his best physically.

"That was getting to know Mardy," Kelly said. "What we tried to do was to get him to understand that I want Mardy on Saturday, but if you can give me something on Tuesday, I can help you get to the NFL. He didn't understand the preparation and how that was going to help him in the NFL. And that's what I was trying to tell him, that I'm doing this to help you get to the next level.

"Mardy is who he is," Kelly continued. "He wears his emotions on his sleeve. He's going to say what he thinks and apologize for it later, which I do not have a problem with. That's just who he is. He loves to play and he loves to play with his teammates. When you get a guy who loves to play and loves to play with his teammates they're going to deal with all the other stuff. Maybe he runs his jaw a little too much at times, but guys are going to look past that when you have such a passion for the game."

Kelly said he had a "great relationship" with Gilyard, and maybe he did at the time, but Gilyard was very critical of Kelly when I talked to him for this book. Maybe that's because he's never forgiven him for leaving for Notre Dame. Or maybe he's always felt that way. Only Gilyard knows for sure.

"I never really fully bought into Brian Kelly," Gilyard said. "Coach D kind of spoiled us. He cared about us as people. BK was totally opposite. We were blue-collar guys. He was a little different. Me and him really bumped heads. He really got on my ass and I really got on his ass. But he gave me my first taste of what it was like having an NFL coach. That's a business. For BK, it was all about, 'Everybody loves a winner.' Coach Kelly was a great head coach. You can't take that away from him."

Gilyard was the number one receiver on the team, but Binns wasn't far behind. During Binns' first two years at Cincinnati, Gilyard was the starter and Binns was his backup. When Dominick

Armon Binns compared his relationship with Gilyard to that of Batman and Robin.

Goodman completed his eligibility in 2008, Binns became a starter alongside Gilyard.

They became such a dynamic tandem that defenses were at a loss to figure out how to deal with them. As the season progressed, foes began to figure they would double-team Gilyard and take their chances against Binns, often to their detriment.

Gilyard finished the season with 87 catches for 1,191 yards and 11 touchdowns, all of which led the Big East, while averaging 13.79 yards per catch. Binns caught 61 passes for 888 yards and also had 11 touchdown catches while averaging 14.6 yards per catch. Factor in Woods (51 catches, 640 yards) and the tight end trio of Guidugli, Alli and Robinson, who combined for 39 catches for 604 yards, and it's easy to understand why the offense was so formidable.

But it all started with Gilyard and Binns.

"We were like Batman and Robin," Binns said. "It was so cool because me and him were roommates on the road ever since my freshman year. I got to talk to him and pick his brain about what goes on out there during a game, how different it is from practice."

Binns was quiet and didn't like doing interviews, so he was content to let Gilyard carry the load in that regard. Gilyard was happy to oblige.

"He was boisterous with a big personality," Binns said. "He was the face of the program. There was a lot of responsibility showing up every day and putting it on like he did. I got to be a kid playing ball. There wasn't the pressure of being the guy."

Many of the players spent time working in the community, but none more than Gilyard, who worked tirelessly in the after-school program at Wesley Chapel in the inner-city neighborhood of Over-the-Rhine. One week he collected coats and sweaters from his teammates and dropped them off at the chapel. Becky Costello, who helped run the after-school program, called Gilyard "a really good role model" when I interviewed her for a story on him that year. Working with inner-city neighborhood kids came naturally to Gilyard.

He was arrested for possessing drugs on a school campus in Bunnell, Florida, an automatic felony. He pleaded guilty, was sent to an alternative school, and did 200 hours of community service in exchange for having the felony expunged from his record.

He had a way with kids, who responded to him because of his playful personality. In a 2008 game against South Florida at Nippert

Stadium, Gilyard ran into the corner of the end zone to catch a pass. He came down with the ball, but was ruled out of bounds. His momentum carried him into the seats where he collided with seven-year-old Garrett Monroe, whose face was painted in Cincinnati's colors of red and black. Before returning to the field, Gilyard paused to check on the youngster. He pulled off his helmet, put his arms around Garrett, gently lifted him out of his seat, and gave him a hug.

Gilyard did not hold back when he talked to reporters, which made him a media favorite. There was no spouting of clichés or toeing the coach's party line for him. He might have engaged in hyperbole at times, but he wasn't phony. What we saw from Gilyard during interviews was the same thing his teammates saw in their interactions with him.

"He was one of my favorite teammates of all-time at any level," said defensive back Brad Jones. "Just the things that Mardy would do and say in practice and on game day were unbelievable. He was almost like a cartoon character."

After his senior year at Cincinnati, Gilyard was named the Big East Special Teams Player of the Year. He was a first-team all-conference selection as a kick returner and wide receiver. His 87 catches in 2009 were the most in school history before Shaq Washington surpassed him with 90 in 2015. He holds the top two marks for most receiving yardage in a season (1,276 in 2008 and 1,191 in 2009).

He ranks second in career receptions with 204, first in career receiving yards with 3,003, and second in career touchdown receptions with 25 (behind Chris Moore's 26). He ranks first in kickoff return yards (2,657), average yards per kickoff (28.6) and kickoff returns for touchdowns (four). And he holds the record for most all-purpose yards in one season -- 2,280 in 2008.

With that kind of production, it's easy to understand why Gilyard wanted an occasional day off for practice and why Pike and his teammates were OK with it.

"I used to tell myself, 'When I leave this place they're going to talk about me for years to come,'" Gilyard said. "That was all the motivation I needed to do anything. It was a hell of a ride. There might have been (Cincinnati) teams that won more (there weren't), but they didn't do what we did for the city. We were trendsetters."

The St. Louis Rams picked Gilyard in the fourth round of the 2010 NFL draft. His NFL career consisted of 19 games for the Rams, the New York Jets and the Philadelphia Eagles. He caught eight passes for 78 yards and no touchdowns. He later played in the Canadian Football League and is still playing professionally for the Massachusetts Pirates of the National Arena League.

"The thing I loved about Mardy," Binns said, "and what was fun about playing with him, is when those lights came on, that dude turned it on. He had confidence that was different from anybody I've ever been around. He was electric."

14

Pike Returns

While Collaros continued to put up big numbers and the Cincinnati offense kept cranking out touchdowns at a ridiculous rate, Pike quietly went about the lonely and tedious business of rehabbing with the help of Colosimo and Mangine, who worked with him every day early in the morning and sometimes late at night. In addition, Mangine insisted that Pike practice falling down every day before he would be allowed back on the field, so that when he did get knocked down in a game he would instinctively know how to protect his injured left arm as he fell to the ground.

Pike felt ridiculous doing it, but he wanted to play, so he did what he was told.

"I was literally practicing as I fell to tuck my arm and my shoulder and fall that way without bracing myself," Pike said. "It was hard and I felt stupid doing it, because the team is down doing special teams practice or team drills, and I'm down there in the end zone with Bob Mangine practicing how to fall. I would just move around and he would say, 'Roll or fall,' and I'd hit the ground. I would probably fall 20 to 30 times, get back up and do it again. But I wouldn't have had a chance to play without Bob Mangine or Dr. Colosimo."

Pike was just one of many Cincinnati players over the years who left the school feeling they owed Mangine a debt of gratitude for what he did to help them overcome an injury. He was more than a trainer. Mangine was also a link to Kelly when the Cincinnati coach needed to know what was going on with the players that perhaps he couldn't see.

"He was a rock to that program," Kelly said. "He was a consistent consigliere. He gave you great insight into players in terms of where their psyche was, their morale. He was so close to the players and understanding them and how they were ticking. He's so much into the mental performance pieces. He was instrumental in the success of that 2009 team."

As the November 13 game against 23rd-ranked West Virginia at Nippert Stadium approached, Pike was close to returning. It couldn't happen soon enough to suit him.

Ever since the Bearcats had joined the Big East in 2005, West Virginia was considered the program they had to beat to win a championship. The Mountaineers played big-time college football in Morgantown's 60,000-seat Milan Puskar Stadium, which they filled or came close to filling every week. Back in the days when Cincinnati tried to survive as an independent, before Conference USA was born, the Bearcats attempted to grow their program by playing occasional games against national powers such as Alabama, Auburn, Miami (Fla.), Penn State, and yes, West Virginia. They would receive a big paycheck for playing on the road and could then sell recruits on the benefits of playing against some of the best competition in the country.

Unfortunately, those games usually resulted in lopsided Cincinnati losses. Sometimes the Bearcats also absorbed injuries that limited them for the rest of the season. The worst of the losses occurred in 1991, 81-0, at Penn State. (They had upset the Nittany Lions, 14-3, in 1983.) The Bearcats lost, 70-21, at Florida State and 45-7 at Alabama in 1990. They played at West Virginia in 1989, Tim Murphy's first of five years as Cincinnati's head coach, and lost, 69-3, a year after falling to the Mountaineers, 51-13, at Cincinnati's Riverfront Stadium.

In the Bearcats' first two games against West Virginia in the Big East, they lost, 38-0 and 42-24. They narrowed the gap in 2007 -- Kelly's first year -- losing 28-23 when the Mountaineers were ranked fifth in the country, and they finally got over the hump in 2008 with a 26-23 overtime win in Morgantown. But playing against West Virginia was still a big deal for Cincinnati, and Pike didn't want to miss the chance to face the Mountaineers one last time at Nippert during his senior year.

There was no announcement before the game that Pike would be able to play. In fact, Collaros was penciled in as the starter just as he had been against Louisville, Syracuse and Connecticut. But Kelly had a secret plan to get Pike back on the field.

Actually, it wasn't that secret. Kelly said earlier in that week that Collaros would start his fourth consecutive game, but that Pike would also play. Of course, the Cincinnati coach wanted to keep the Mountaineers guessing to some extent, so he didn't disclose that Pike

Tony Pike returned to start against Illinois and threw a school-record six touchdown passes.

would play only when the Bearcats got into the red zone. He did point out that Collaros' superb play gave him the luxury to not have to rush Pike back into action to save the season. Clearly that wasn't an issue.

But he did want to make sure that when Pike came back, he would be the same Tony Pike who had played so well before he was injured. One more game with Collaros starting would make that more likely, especially with a bye week looming after the West Virginia game.

On a Friday night, in a game televised on ESPN2 and played before a Nippert Stadium record crowd of 35,105, Kelly unleashed Pike on the fifth-ranked Bearcats' first possession. After Collaros completed a pass to Guidugli for 18 yards to the West Virginia 10-

yard line, Pike trotted onto the field to replace Collaros. His first pass in almost a month resulted in a 10-yard touchdown to Binns, which gave the Bearcats a 7-0 lead. He threw another TD pass on the Bearcats' first possession of the third quarter. Again, Collaros drove Cincinnati down the field, this time completing a 22-yard pass to Woods that put the ball on the Mountaineers' six-yard line.

In came Pike again to finish off the drive. His first two passes -- one intended for Guidugli, the other for Pead -- were incomplete. But on third-and-goal, he threw to Woods for a six-yard touchdown that gave the Bearcats a 21-14 lead with 11:07 left in the third quarter.

West Virginia started on its 20-yard line with 11:24 remaining in the fourth quarter, still trailing by seven, and drove from its 20 to the Cincinnati 24. The Bearcats' defense surrendered 202 rushing yards to the Mountaineers that night. But on fourth-and-eight, the defense came up with another big play with the outcome still very much in doubt. When quarterback Jarrett Brown dropped back to pass, Curtis Young forced Brown to hurry the pass for an incompletion. Cincinnati took over on downs, Pead ran for 43 yards, and Rogers kicked a 38-yard field goal, which gave the Bearcats a 24-14 lead with 2:08 to play.

The Mountaineers went 64 yards in seven plays to cut the Cincinnati lead to three with 39 seconds remaining. Binns then snagged the onside kick and Collaros took a knee to seal the 24-21 Cincinnati victory. The win gave the Bearcats a 10-0 record for the first time in school history. West Virginia fell to 3-2 in the league,

7-3 overall, and was eliminated from Big East title contention.

Pike finished the game with two completions in four attempts for 16 yards and two touchdowns. Collaros was outstanding again, going 17-for-24 for 205 yards with one interception. But it was Pike who stole the show with his dramatic appearances.

After the game, Pike talked as if he had been surprised that Kelly sent him into the game when the Bearcats reached the red zone.

"When we got to the red zone, (Kelly) said, 'Pike!' I was just kind of following along on the sideline," Pike said. "I thought he was calling me to talk about a play or something. He told me to go in. I kind of had some trouble getting my chin strap buttoned."

In fact, using Pike in those situations had been the Bearcats' plan all along.

"We were trying to find ways to insert somebody that had such a different skill set," Kelly said, "a player who was six-six, can really scan the field, and was extremely effective and patient in the red zone. I don't know that I've ever had a quarterback that has been as effective and efficient in the red zone throwing the ball as well as Tony Pike because of his vision and patience. He was Tom Brady-like in a sense down there. So that's how we kind of rolled with it, inserting him into games to get the most production into the offense."

"We knew West Virginia had a really good red zone defense," Pike said. "My arm wasn't healed enough to play every down and take hits. But because I was a taller quarterback, we knew coming in that if we had red zone opportunities I would come in. Then it was either, hey, if it's there, make the throw. If not, throw it out of bounds."

After the game, Pike saluted Collaros for being a good teammate and not complaining about being taken out of the game even though it might have cost him two more touchdown passes. Collaros was magnanimous as he played the role of good soldier at the time by not complaining publicly, but he admits now that he wasn't happy about it. Really, what quarterback wouldn't have been upset?

"I definitely took it personally," Collaros said. "I wasn't mad at Tony. There was obviously a reason for it. Our coaching staff thought that whatever set of plays we ran down there were better suited for Tony. But yeah, I took it personally. Anybody in that situation who claims they didn't is lying to you. But we won the game, right? So it's all good."

Pike's return was the story of the game, but it just as easily could have been Pead's 175-yard rushing performance on 18 carries. At the time, the yardage was his career high.

It was Pead's first career start. In one sense, he said it wasn't a major change for him, except for the distinction of becoming a starter, because even as a backup he prided himself on preparing well for each game. The only difference was that now he was running with the first team all week during practice. He remembers getting some pointed advice from Kelly that week.

"We were practicing a play," he said. "It was a sweep or

something. Coach Kelly kept telling me that when I got the ball I was going to be one-on-one with the corner. It was a short field and I was running toward the boundary. 'You've got to make him miss,' he said. Sure enough, he called the play and it was just me one-on-one with the corner, number eight. I hit him with the boop-boop (move). I didn't score. I tripped and fell. But I did make him miss."

Collaros had played so well that at least among Cincinnati fans there was a question about who should start in the next game against Illinois. The Cincinnati Enquirer conducted a poll of its readers, who chose Collaros over Pike by a vote of 1,132 to 1,117. Of course none of those votes meant anything to Kelly, who decided to go back to Pike when he was healthy, or at least healthy enough to play.

Kelly told reporters that Collaros was making it difficult to automatically start Pike, but in the end he chose the more experienced Pike to ride the Bearcats to the finish line of what was still a perfect season. Kelly liked Pike's height, his strong arm and the body of work he had produced over a longer period of time. When the decision was made Collaros was disappointed, but not surprised.

"I knew what the deal was," Collaros said. "When Tony was healthy he was going to play. He was having an unbelievable season. I just knew I had to make the most of the opportunity I was given while I was out there."

Until Pike was injured, Collaros had never been told that he was number two on the depth chart ahead of Anderson. In his mind, they were 2a and 2b and he didn't know if he was 'a' or 'b', so he

Pike wore a brace on his left arm when he returned to action.

always felt that he had to prove himself.

As he looks back now on Kelly's decision, he understands even better why Kelly had little choice but to return to Pike.

"I've been on the other end of that now that my (Canadian Football League) career has gone a little further," Collaros said. "I've been hurt, and the backup has done well, but I've come back and played afterward. But it was still a little weird."

For Kelly, the decision must have been like a tycoon trying to decide which car to take out for a spin on a Sunday afternoon. Should he take the Rolls or the Bentley? He knew he couldn't go wrong either way. At the time, Pike was 128-for-199 (64.3 percent) for 1,633 yards and 15 touchdowns with three interceptions for a passer efficiency rating of 155.11 (a rating of 100-plus is considered excellent). Collaros was 76 of 100 (76.0 percent) for 1,299 yards with 10 touchdowns with one interception. His rating was 210.24.

Pike would have to play with a brace on his left arm, but he wasn't worried about doing any further damage.

"I figured I'd deal with the pain later," he said.

There was plenty to deal with. When fans see football players play hurt, they praise them for having courage or guts. They admire their toughness. Mostly they're just happy to have them back on the field because they want their team to win. They don't think very much about the risks involved or the pain those players have to endure.

But that pain is real. To get through the game, Pike received a shot of Toradol, a non-steroidal anti-inflammatory drug.

"I wouldn't have been able to play without it," Pike said. "Once you play with Toradol, yes, I didn't feel any pain in my arm. But you also don't feel the hits that you take, so once the Toradol wears off you feel it everywhere. But you're not thinking about 10 years down the road. You're thinking about the opportunities at hand. It was miserable. I would get back into rehab the next day with ice and stem (treatments). Now that I've gotten older, I have pain in that arm, but I would go back and do the same thing again."

It wasn't until after the regular season, during the nearly month-long break before the Sugar Bowl, that Pike felt his body was back to normal.

Pike didn't find out he would start against Illinois until the day before the November 27 game after another bye week. He and Collaros divided first-team reps pretty evenly throughout the week leading up to the game. But Pike was determined to make the most of his final appearance at Nippert. It was Senior Day, all his friends and family members would be on hand, and the Bearcats were

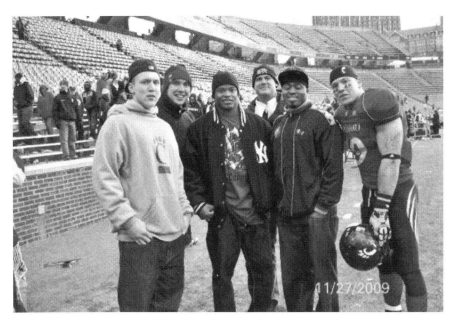
Ben Guidugli, far right, caught two of the six touchdowns passes that Tony Pike threw against Illinois to break the school record set by Ben's brother, Gino, second from left. Also pictured from left to right are Tony Guidugli and former UC players Tyjaun Hagler, Kyle Takavitz and Cedric Dawley.

facing a Big Ten opponent.

He had spent the first half of his college career wearing a cap and holding a clipboard on the sideline, knowing there was virtually no chance that he would play. Now he was finishing his career as one of the best quarterbacks in Cincinnati history. Not only did he play, he went out in spectacular fashion, completing 32 of 46 passes for 399 yards and six touchdown passes in the fifth-ranked Bearcats' 49-36 win over the Illini (3-8), improving Cincinnati's record to 11-0.

"I took a hit early in the game," Pike said. "Taking that hit and feeling fine afterward was the green light, because you still have that mental block, that 'OK, if I fall, is something else going to happen?' Once you fall and you clear that, you're just playing football and playing free. That was a game where everything went right. The game plan came together and everyone on offense did his job."

Pike's six touchdown passes broke the school record of five, which was set by Gino Guidugli against Southern Miss in a 52-24 Cincinnati win over 21st-ranked Southern Miss in 2004. Two of Pike's TD passes were to Gino's brother, Ben, the Bearcats' tight end, who caught seven passes overall for a career-high 149 yards.

"That was like a dream come true," Ben said. "Gino was at the game. I think I had my picture taken with him after the game."

Guidugli was one of four Cincinnati receivers who caught seven passes against the Illini. The others were Gilyard (102 yards, two touchdowns), Binns (62 yards, two touchdowns) and Woods (53 yards, 1 touchdown). The Bearcats ran for only 21 yards on 15 carries. Not that it mattered.

Collaros never got in the game. In fact, he didn't throw another pass the rest of the season. During the next two years playing under Butch Jones he blossomed into a great quarterback in his own right. He holds the school record for career completion percentage (62.4), ranks 10th in passing yards (4,338), ninth in yards per completion (13.59), and sixth in touchdown passes (36). He was first-team all-Big East in 2010 and second-team in 2011.

He's played seven seasons in the CFL for Toronto, Hamilton and now Saskatchewan, passing for 16,285 yards and 92 touchdowns. He won a Grey Cup championship with 2012 with Toronto.

It's possible that none of that would have happened if it weren't for the 2009 season at Cincinnati when he got his chance to prove he could be a top-flight quarterback and made the most of it.

"We had an amazing group of people working together to achieve the goals that we set," Collaros said. "I have life-long friends from that team. Personally, that season helped put me on the map, especially the South Florida game and the Connecticut game. The people in Toronto watched those games and said, 'He can play up here.'"

15

Pike to Binns

The Bearcats' locker room at halftime of the Pittsburgh game was filled with conflicting emotions. There's no doubt that Gilyard's kickoff return had provided the team with reason to hope for the second half, but their problems weren't over, not by a long shot. They still trailed Pitt by two touchdowns, their star quarterback was still struggling, and their defense still hadn't found a way to contain Lewis.

Some players were angry about the way they had played in the first half. Others feared that their perfect season was about to come to an end. They had just 20 minutes to regroup before the start of the second half. The players had to get their heads straight. The coaches had to strategize. And everybody needed to calm down.

"We came into the locker room, all the coaches went into the office, and there was yelling and screaming going on in the players' locker room," Kelly said. "I remember Kerry Coombs leaving the coaches' locker room and coming back and saying, 'Mardy's going crazy in here. You need to come in here.'

"So I walked in, and Mardy was up in arms about how nobody was holding up their end of the bargain. I said, 'You've got to settle down. You take care of what you can take care of.' He was animated to the point where he was sweating."

Gilyard was upset mainly because the Bearcats weren't playing the way he was accustomed to seeing them play.

"They don't have nothin' over here in Pittsburgh," Gilyard said. "They shouldn't even have got to this point. Now we really got to play. I went to Pike and I said, 'I have faith in you. I don't know what's going on, but we can't do this without you, period.' He stood up and apologized for the way he played in the first half."

Collaros was waiting in the wings in case Kelly decided that Pike just didn't have it that day. Kelly considered making the switch, but decided to stick with Pike.

"Our best chance was Tony," Kelly said. "It wasn't the kind of game that Zach excels at, coming from behind. It was a Tony Pike kind of game. We needed him to snap out of it."

While Pike was gathering himself for the second half, his parents were moving to different seats. They ended up in a private box, where they watched the second half with Steelers quarterback Ben Roethlisberger. Pike's not sure how they got in there, but he believes an NFL agent with a connection to Roethlisberger arranged for the move.

"Agents try to contact you during the season," Pike said. "I told my parents, 'I'm not talking to anyone during the season. You guys meet with them and pick your top three or four and let me know.' I'm sure the most pleasant things weren't being said in the UC fan section. And the fact that Zach had come in and done such a good job, there probably were a lot of people wanting me out of the game. I think my parents moved because they just got stressed out. They could never sit still, especially when I wasn't playing well."

The Bearcats went back onto the field for the second half, determined to make the most of the final 30 minutes. Gilyard's return had given them a chance. Now they had to capitalize on it.

That didn't happen right away. Pittsburgh got the ball to start the second half and the Cincinnati defense did exactly what it needed to do, forcing a three-and-out and keeping the momentum from quickly shifting back to the Panthers. But when Pike and the offense went out for their first possession of the second half, it seemed as if nothing had changed. Pike's first pass to Gilyard was incomplete. Then he was sacked for a loss of five yards. On third-and-15, he ran for a 15-yard loss and fumbled the ball, which he recovered himself. Rogers entered the game to punt.

At that juncture, there was no sign that the Bearcats had figured out anything on offense. But apparently they did on defense. After Rogers' punt, Pitt took over on its 25-yard line. The Panthers were called for holding on the first play of the possession. Ray Graham gained 13 yards to the Pitt 45, but the Bearcats held from there and forced a second punt in as many second-half possessions for the Panthers.

"We were doing some different things in the second half," Diaco said. "They showed themselves and gave us an opportunity to put a hat on spots that we hadn't done in the first half and we got them slowed."

Then Cincinnati's offense came alive. On second-and-14 from the Bearcats' 32, Gilyard made another big play, a 68-yard touchdown pass from Pike. Rogers' extra-point kick drew the Bearcats to within seven points at 31-24 with 8:12 remaining in the third quarter. The momentum now had swung completely in Cincinnati's favor.

Pitt coach Wannstedt had gambled successfully during the first half by guarding against the long pass in the hope that the Bearcats wouldn't settle for the underneath passes. But now in the second half, the Bearcats were poised to take advantage of what the defense was giving them.

"We made some adjustments," Kelly said. "They were playing off coverage and dropping eight into coverage. That's when we started to pick them apart with a lot of drives and crosses. We just methodically started to go down the field patiently."

"We went back to what we did," Pike said, "possession by possession, play by play, knowing that we can score quick, we can move the ball quick, knowing that now we're not counting possessions."

After Rogers' kickoff, Pitt started its next drive at its seven-yard line. Again, the Cincinnati defense held, thanks in large part to a 10-yard sack of Stull by Schaffer at the 17, which forced the Panthers to punt again. But Pike was intercepted for the third time on the Bearcats' next possession when he tried to hit Gilyard at Pitt's 17-yard line.

The third quarter ended with the Panthers still holding a 31-

24 lead. On the first play of the fourth quarter, Cincinnati's Dominique Battle intercepted a Stull pass on the Bearcats' seven. After three incomplete passes by Pike, the Bearcats were forced to punt again. Pitt took over on the Cincinnati 32 and needed only four Lewis carries for gains of four, four, nine, and finally 15 yards for a touchdown. Hutchins' extra point increased Pitt's lead back to 14 points at 38-24 with 12:26 remaining.

Time was running out on the Bearcats' perfect season. But then Gilyard came up with another big return, taking the Panthers' kickoff and returning it 49 yards to the Pitt 23. On first-and-goal from the eight, Pike hooked up with Woods for an eight-yard touchdown pass. But Rogers' extra point kick was no good when holder Collaros had trouble handling Windt's snap, the ball getting pinned against Collaros' right leg, which disrupted Rogers' timing. His kick glanced off the right upright. Still, the Bearcats were within one touchdown of the Panthers, trailing 38-30 with 11:09 to play.

"I can't point any blame at anybody," Rogers said of the missed extra point. "It was just an operational issue. We just didn't click on all cylinders on that. It's me who missed it, so I'll take the heat."

With 5:46 remaining, Cincinnati tied the score at 38-38 on a seven-play, 68-yard touchdown drive that ended with Pead's one-yard run. Pike then passed to Gilyard for the two-point conversion.

The Panthers reclaimed the lead on Lewis' five-yard touchdown run with 1:38 left, but holder Andrew Janocko, a sophomore backup quarterback, bobbled the snap, preventing

Hutchins from making the extra-point kick, and providing the Bearcats with the opening they needed. They trailed by only six, 44-38.

"Everything that we did to try to get the momentum back, it didn't work," Wannstedt said. "And then, at the end of the game, we fumble a snap. It's icy and snowy. He mishandles it. So again, that's another momentum opportunity that we lose."

The Cincinnati offense was huddled on the sideline, getting ready to go back onto the field when they saw Pitt had botched the extra point. The Panthers still led, 44-38, but the Bearcats knew that a touchdown and an extra point could win the game.

"There was nothing said. There was just a look," Pike said. "You could just tell that everyone knew what was going to happen. All of sudden, it was now we can go win this game. That changed everything. We'd done this a million times in practice and in games."

The Bearcats began their final drive at their 39-yard line after Gilyard returned the kickoff 26 yards. Almost as if on automatic pilot, Pike passed to Gilyard for seven yards to the Cincinnati 46. He passed to Woods for 10 yards to the Pitt 44. On first-and-10, he threw again to Gilyard, who was cutting across the middle, to the Pitt 29.

"I was pushed out of the pocket rolling out right," Pike said. "They tell quarterbacks to never throw back across your body over the middle, but I had seen Mardy break off his route and come back over the middle. I was able to make a throw to him, which got us in position."

The Bearcats called timeout with 29 seconds remaining. The Panthers feared Gilyard so much at that point that they altered their defensive structure in an attempt to prevent him from making still another big play. It turned out to be a big mistake. As Pike approached the line of scrimmage, he noticed that Pitt was cheating a safety toward Gilyard, leaving Binns one-on-one with cornerback Jovani Chappel.

"Armon for much of the second half of the year was the go-to guy," Pike said, "but Mardy in that game had been so electric with the kickoff return and the receiving touchdown and the two-point conversion. So even though a lot of times teams would play base even coverage, toward the end of the game they were rotating a safety to Mardy's side to kind of double-team Mardy.

"I don't know exactly what play was called, but as we broke the huddle we lined up so quick that teams couldn't hide their defense. The safety was already rotating to Mardy's side, and I knew on the backside they were in man-to-man on Armon. I don't care who the corner would be, I would take Armon one-on-one against anyone in the country. I signaled to Binns to change his route to a fade. From then, I knew I had it. The first three steps I had to look to the left to hold the safety. There was no turning back to see if Armon's there. It was just knowing that he was going to beat his guy. From there, it was pitch and catch."

Binns knew "a go route" was always an option depending on the coverage. Anytime Pike saw that he had one-on-one coverage on Binns, he could check the play at the line of scrimmage. So as soon as Pike gave Binns the signal, he knew the ball was coming to him. Then it was up to him to beat Chappel, who was from Dayton, Ohio, about an hour drive up I-75 from Cincinnati. At 5-foot-9, Chappel was surrendering six inches to the 6-foot-3 Binns.

"He was a pretty physical guy," Binns said. "He wasn't real tall, but he was strong. He was a stocky kid. He was pretty good at the point of attack, so they used him on the short side of the field and that's usually where I was, so we were matched up the majority of the game. Mardy had been doing it to everybody all year long. You kind of had to pick your poison, and Mardy was the more established guy at that time because he had started the whole year before. They felt like they would take the chance and leave everybody else in one-on-one matchups."

Binns made a quick step inside against Chappel to keep him off his back, then headed toward the right sideline. As Pike prepared to throw the ball in Binns' direction, he could see that Binns had Chappel beaten by a step or two. He knew all he had to do was get the ball over Chappel's head. Binns would take care of the rest. He didn't have to worry about the safety showing up to intercept it, but he had to make sure he didn't under throw it, which could have given Chappel a chance to swat it away or pick it off.

He took two steps back, then moved up in the pocket and lofted the ball perfectly over Binns' left shoulder. Chappel fell down as the ball dropped into Binns' hands, his arms slightly extended. As Binns caught the ball with 33 seconds left, his momentum carried him to the ground in the end zone. He rolled over, then he held the

Armon Binns completes the game-tying touchdown catch against Pitt and falls into the end zone while protecting the ball.

ball up for all to see as the Cincinnati fans erupted in celebration.

Here's how Dan Hoard, the long-time play-by-play radio broadcaster for Cincinnati, described the catch for his WLW-AM listeners: *"Twenty-three-year-old Tony Pike waits for the snap, has the football, short drop, lofts one down the sideline for Binns. He's got it! Touchdown! Touchdown! Touchdown! Armon Binns catches a perfect throw. There's a penalty flag back at the 30-yard line. It's on Pitt. Touchdown!"*

Pike pumped his fist into the air as he danced his way down the field toward Binns with the score tied at 44-44.

"In the moment, I wasn't thinking about anything but catching that football," Binns said. "I was always taught to look up in the air for deep balls, but don't look back toward the quarterback, so I looked up and I tried to find the tip of the football and just focus on it all the way in. It was such a beautiful throw, man. He hit me right in stride. I didn't have to overextend.

"It was so sloshy, that field. That Pittsburgh stadium field, even on good days, can be a little hectic. I was just trying to keep my balance. I didn't know how close the cornerback was, but I knew he stumbled a little bit. The whole play he was right there trying to grab on my arm. I was just trying to make sure I held onto it and protected it when I caught it."

When Pike saw the penalty flag, he initially thought the call was offensive holding, which would have wiped out the touchdown, but it was offside on Pitt defensive end Greg Romeus, the Big East co-defensive player of the year. It wasn't until Pike watched the film later that he noticed Cincinnati left tackle Jeff Linkenbach had still

Jeff Linkenbach, who made the key block that allowed Tony Pike to throw the pass to Armon Binns, celebrates with Binns, Ben Guidugli and Sam Griffin.

managed to block Romeus, even though he was offside, giving Pike the time he needed to push into the pocket and make the throw.

"Jeff Linkenbach holding that block long enough is just as big a part of that play as Armon making the catch," Pike said.

Pike had come a long way. Two years earlier, Kelly had felt

compelled to confront him in the dining room at Camp Higher Ground and issue an ultimatum to get him to reach his potential. During Pike's first year as a starter, he was frequently reamed out on the sideline by Kelly for not making what Kelly thought was the correct read. Now, with an undefeated season on the line, he had made the adjustment at the line of scrimmage that resulted in the biggest touchdown pass in Cincinnati football history.

"That was Tony Pike," Kelly said. "He would take what he was given. He was really an extension of what I could see from the sideline. He was the coach on the field. He made the right check. He deserves a lot of credit there, certainly."

Ten years later, Wannstedt still questions his decision to shift the safety to double Gilyard.

"We knew we were in a mismatch there with Chappel," Wannstedt said. "We had been playing Aaron Berry, who played in the NFL, locking up on Gilyard. He was doing a heck of a job, so I felt good about that. But at the end of the game, rather than play zone and help out the undersized corner, we played man and we tried rushing four. Our guy was there. He wasn't fooled. He wasn't tripped. Pike made a great throw and Binns made a great catch. You always second-guess yourself as a coach. We left the kid alone. It was not his fault. He was physically in a mismatch."

There was so much joy among Cincinnati's players and fans after Binns' catch that it seemed the Bearcats had already won. But there was still the matter of Rogers kicking the extra point, which was anything but automatic in this game, each team having already

Jake Rogers kicks the game-winning extra point against Pitt.

failed to convert one of its attempts.

"When we went out, I told Mike Windt, 'Let's get this snapped,'" Rogers said. "I told Zach, 'Just get the ball down and I'll kick it. I promise.' I think it was probably a pretty slow operation, but I was sure when the ball went down that I was going to put it through."

This time the snap was true, the hold was perfect, and Rogers' kick sailed through the uprights.

"I still get goose bumps when I watch that game," Rogers said. "It's just an unreal feeling. I didn't think that I hit the game-winner, I thought, 'Holy crap, our team just came back from a deficit and came through for the win.'"

Cincinnati led by one point with 33 seconds to play. All that remained was for the Bearcats' defense to keep the Panthers from making a last-ditch push into field goal territory.

Rogers kicked off to Pitt's Ray Graham, who managed to get back only to the 18-yard line, where he was run out of bounds by Charley Howard. With time running out, Lewis' running was largely neutralized at that point. The Panthers had no choice but to pass and hope for a breakdown in the Cincinnati secondary. But Stull's three passes -- intended for Cedric McGee, Dorin Dickerson, and Baldwin -- all fell incomplete. On fourth-and-10, Stull dropped back for his final pass only to be sacked by Daniels with three seconds remaining.

The Cincinnati offense came back on the field and Pike took a knee to kill the final seconds. The Bearcats were Big East champs for the second straight year. They had overcome the weather, the Heinz Field crowd, Lewis' running ability, and their own spotty play in the first half. They were headed for their second straight appearance in a BCS bowl game, having completed the first perfect regular season (12-0) in school history.

"In the second half, our defense, we totally turned it around," Daniels said. "It wasn't what the coaches did. It was what the players did. We got together and we said we're not going out like this. All we kept saying is, 'We're not going to a shitty bowl. We're going to the BCS.'"

The Bearcats had outscored, Pitt 28-13, in the second half to post a 45-44 victory.

Lewis ran for 194 yards and three touchdowns on 47 carries.

Pike finished 22-for-44 for 302 yards and three touchdowns, with three interceptions. After an abysmal first half, he went 14-for-21 in the second half for 218 yards, and two touchdowns with one interception. Pead gained 76 yards on nine carries with one

touchdown. Woods led the Bearcats in catches with seven for 61 yards and one touchdown. Gilyard caught five passes for 118 yards with one touchdown

Mardy Gilyard joins the Cincinnati fans in celebration of the Bearcats' come-from-behind win over Pitt.

and finished with 381 all-purpose yards. And Binns caught five passes for 104 yards and the game-winning touchdown. The Cincinnati defense held Pitt to 137 yards in the second half.

"That game stands by itself as the most unbelievable football game I've ever watched in my life," said Jim Kelly Jr., Hoard's partner in the radio booth.

After Binns got up off the Heinz Field turf, the first person he saw was Guidugli.

"I didn't have time to react to anything because he tackled me," Binns said. "Eventually Sam Griffin and everybody started piling up. The moment got so emotional to come back like that in a game that meant so much. There's a picture of me, Mardy and D.J. all huddled up. We were so passionate. We put so much into it. It was so special with the type of year we were having."

The handshake line was quiet after the game. The Panthers had to be in shock over what had just happened, and the Bearcats did their best to keep from gloating. There had been little taunting during the game.

Moments later, the same Cincinnati locker room that had been the scene of so much passionate angst a few hours earlier was awash in emotion of a different kind.

"It was all celebration," Pike said. "Brian Kelly was in there celebrating with us. We sang the fight song like we did after every game. The talk in the locker room was that we had done something that no one could ever take from us. Brian Kelly came up and gave me a hug and told me how proud he was of me. These were emotional times, because there's so much on the field and you're sharing that moment with teammates and friends and family. You're doing it on someone else's field, which makes it even more special. You erased a 21-point deficit. There was just that relief that we did something that had never happened at UC before."

Kelly told the players in the locker room that he was honored to be their coach. Notre Dame had fired Weis five days earlier, and speculation about his replacement had continued to focus on Kelly. When he arrived at his post-game press conference, he was immediately asked about a report on ABC-TV during the game that said he had agreed to talk to Notre Dame officials about their coaching vacancy.

Reporters were simply doing their job, which Kelly should have understood. But the Cincinnati coach didn't like the question and lashed out at reporters for overlooking what he and his team had just accomplished.

"I'm not going to talk about my job situation," he said. "If anybody else wants to ask a question, here's the response you'll get. Let's talk about back-to-back championship teams and these kids. That's the focus. It's going to be on these kids. There is more misinformation out there and you folks need to get a handle on it because it's ridiculous."

Kelly remembered his outburst.

"I was angry," he said, "because I wanted to enjoy the moment with our players. That was more important to me than anything else. We had come so far. We had experienced a lot during the season and overcame some adversity. That's what you work for and you want to share it with your players because it goes so fast. It was what you want when you spend 80 hours a week with your team. That's the way you want to finish it."

Coombs and Brad Jones hugged each other when Coombs toted the Big East championship trophy into the locker room.

"My journey of competing and trying to be a starter and be productive, it all ended in winning the Big East championship," Jones said. "I was able to fight with those guys and win. Just getting embraced by Kerry and hugging each other and saying, we did it. It was awesome."

This is What the Top Feels Like

When Pike saw Binns in the locker room, he noticed that his left shoulder was in a sling. He assumed that Binns had injured the shoulder as he fell to the ground after making the game-tying catch. In fact, Binns had hurt his shoulder earlier in the game when Pike threw a pass to him off a fade route in the corner. After making the catch he fell on his shoulder, then the defender fell on top of the shoulder and separated it.

"I tried to block on the next play," Binns said. "I had the most agonizing pain I had ever felt to that point. A little bit before halftime, they took me in and worked on it and got me back on the field. I was able to grind it out. The momentum and everything that goes into that type of game, you're not thinking about injuries at that point. You're just trying to do whatever you can to get back out there. Thankfully, I was able to. I played the whole game. I didn't have a lot of range of motion. I could barely lift my hand over my head. The next morning when I woke up I couldn't even lift my arm to scratch my face."

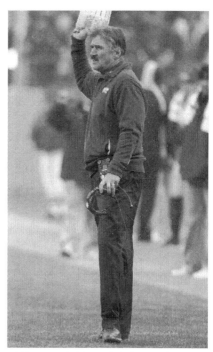

Pitt coach Dave Wannstedt questioned his decision to double-team Mardy Gilyard on the Armon Binns TD catch.

Over in the Pitt locker room, Wannstedt was trying to find the right words for his players after the crushing loss.

"I spun it as fast as I could," he said.

He told the Panthers they still had a chance to post a 10-win season for the first time since 1981 if they could win their upcoming bowl game, which they did, defeating North Carolina, 19-17, in the Meineke Car Care Bowl.

"I just told them, 'You know what? We had a chance to make plays, guys,'" Wannstedt said. "It wasn't any one thing that really let us down. We gave up a play on defense. We gave up a play on special teams. We mishandled a snap. Our players looked in the mirror. The team lost. It wasn't one guy or one play."

There would be more drama before the day was finished. The Bearcats had begun the day ranked No. 4 in the BCS standings, behind No. 3 Texas, No. 2 Alabama, and No. 1 Florida. If everything broke just right elsewhere, they could land a spot in the national championship game.

16

Kelly Says Goodbye

As the Bearcats made their joyful bus ride across I-70 on the way back to Cincinnati, Alabama was in the process of upsetting top-ranked Florida, 32-13, in the Southeastern Conference championship game in the Georgia Dome in Atlanta. A few hours later, the Big 12 Championship game between Texas and Nebraska began to unfold at Cowboys Stadium in Arlington, Texas, and the Cornhuskers appeared poised to knock off the Longhorns.

If that happened, there was a good chance the Bearcats would move past both Florida and Texas into the No. 2 spot in the BCS standings, and earn the right to play No. 1 Alabama for the national championship.

The Bearcats were fully aware of how events were unfolding as they made their way toward the Queen City after their own stirring victory.

"At that point," Pike said, "my thought and the team's thought was that we're playing for the national championship. Texas was ahead of us. They lose. We win. We're going to jump them."

But some of the Cincinnati players didn't believe that could happen, even if Nebraska did hold on to beat Texas. They understood that Cincinnati wasn't one of the elite names in college

175

football and were convinced that somehow the powers that be would find a way to keep them from playing for the national title.

"Honestly, I didn't put much stock in us playing in it," Webster said. "I knew the committee probably would want a bigger (football) school to be in the national championship than Cincinnati."

Webster's skepticism was understandable, but the way the system was set up, it seemed certain that if the Bearcats finished second in the BCS standings they would play for the title, regardless of their lack of pedigree. First, though, Nebraska had to finish the job of knocking off Texas.

After the Bearcats returned to campus, Kelly and Longo headed to Fifth Third Arena on the Cincinnati campus to watch the end of the Texas-Nebraska game. Unlike Webster, Kelly had no doubt that if Nebraska held on to win, the Bearcats would play in the BCS title game.

"I had bought one of the basketball suites and had it redone and it had a nice TV in there," Kelly said. "We watched the last quarter of the game, just the two of us. We looked at it thinking, 'We're going to play for the national championship. This is amazing.' Then the way it finished, it was pretty disappointing."

Trailing 12-10, Texas had the ball on the Nebraska 29-yard line and was facing third-and-13 with eight seconds remaining. Texas quarterback Colt McCoy took the snap from center. With Nebraska's Ndamukong Suh in hot pursuit, he rolled to his right and threw a pass that sailed out of bounds as time expired on the game clock. The Cornhuskers players swarmed the field in celebration.

But their celebration was premature. The officials cleared the field and huddled for a conference, after which they put one second back on the clock. Granted a reprieve, Texas sent kicker Hunter Lawrence onto the field. Lawrence kicked a 46-yard field goal to win the game, 13-12, for the Longhorns. The Bearcats would not be playing for the national title after all.

"We got screwed when they put that damn second back on the clock," Gilyard said. "That game was supposed to be over right there. (McCoy) threw it high and out of bounds. When he throws it high and out of bounds, that ran the clock down to zero."

Three days later, the Oklahoman newspaper reported that the second had been restored because officials ruled that the ball McCoy had thrown out of bounds had hit a part of the stadium -- perhaps a railing -- with one second remaining. The rules dictated that the clock stop at that point.

The Bearcats had been on a high after their comeback victory over Pitt. Their emotions were lifted even higher when it appeared they would play for the national title. Now that prize had been snatched away from them in an abrupt -- and to them unfair -- manner.

"We were really proud of the season that had taken place," Kelce said "It was a great culmination of how far the program had come. We were all hoping we were going to the national championship, but I wouldn't say we were disappointed. We did have a chip on our shoulder and felt a little bit slighted, but I don't

About 1,200 fans showed up at Fifth Third Arena to cheer the Bearcats' announcement that they would play Florida in the Sugar Bowl.

think anybody was disappointed about going to the Sugar Bowl."

The next day, on Sunday, December 6, the Bearcats officially accepted an invitation to play Florida in the Sugar Bowl on January 1 in New Orleans. About 1,200 fans showed up at Fifth Third Arena to watch the BCS Selection Show with the players and the coaching staff.

The Bearcats finished the regular season ranked No. 4 in both the AP media poll and the USA Today coaches' poll, one spot ahead of No. 5 Florida. They finished third in the BCS standings, which all but confirmed that they would have played for the national championship if the officials hadn't restored that second at the end of the Texas-Nebraska game. Instead, Texas played Alabama in the BCS title game, and lost, 37-21.

Kelly said that afternoon he had voted the Bearcats No. 1 in the country on his ballot for the USA Today Top 25.

"Hey, we're 12-0," he said. "Show me why we can't be number one. We won all of our games. After watching Nebraska-Texas last night, I felt we're as good as anybody."

As Kelly walked onto the basketball floor to address the fans,

Fans chanted Brian Kelly's name at the Fifth Third Arena gathering.

they started to chant his name, as if they were trying to show him how much they wanted him to stay. By then the Kelly-to-Notre Dame rumors were raging. I talked to Kelly after the Fifth Third Arena event and asked him if he had talked to anyone from Notre Dame. He assured me that he hadn't, but that didn't mean his agent hadn't been in touch with Notre Dame AD Swarbrick.

Kelly told his players during a bowl logistics meeting the next day that he would talk to Notre Dame about its head coaching job.

He promised them they would be the first to hear about his decision and instructed them to not listen to what the media was saying or writing. He confirmed on his Twitter account that he was to meet with Notre Dame officials on Tuesday, December 8 in New York, where he would be for the National Football Foundation dinner. But that meeting didn't take place until the following day.

Meanwhile, Kelly was also in discussions with Thomas, the Cincinnati athletic director, about a contract extension that would keep him in Cincinnati.

"Cincinnati was ready to put together an awesome contract," Kelly said. "I would have been happy (to stay) because I didn't know what it looked like on the other side anyway. I hadn't swam in those waters. They were on it. They were doing their due diligence and were proactive. They were really good."

Thomas had been involved for some time in raising funds to cover Kelly's latest contract. He estimated the school had raised from five million to six million dollars to cover the cost of Kelly's contract and the contracts of his assistant coaches after he was courted by Tennessee, Washington, and several other schools. But when he saw that Notre Dame was calling, he knew he would have a difficult time keeping Kelly.

"When I got the call from Jack Swarbrick that they were interested in talking to Brian I knew that because it was Notre Dame it was going to take more of an effort," Thomas said. "There were some things we could have continued to do facility-wise to support his program and his staff, but I think at the end of the day, especially when you're dealing with Notre Dame, it would have been a real challenge. Let's face it. He had other BCS schools coming after him. When you have successful coaches, those are the things you have to deal with."

Thomas was unable to say how close Cincinnati came to matching Notre Dame's offer from a financial standpoint because he didn't know what he was bidding against. Kelly was in a position to know what each school was offering, but said money wasn't the main issue for him.

"I had to decide whether Notre Dame was going to be the fit that I was looking for, because I was comfortable with the financial package that Cincinnati was offering," Kelly said. "Here's the bottom line: I was comfortable with what Cincinnati was doing. I felt like they were doing everything to secure my future at Cincinnati, so it wasn't a financial decision. It was, 'Do I want to stay at Cincinnati and continue to build this program, or do I want to take a look at this historic program at Notre Dame?' So money really wasn't the issue. It's just that I knew that Cincinnati had really stepped up."

While all this was going on, the Cincinnati players were left to wonder what was happening. For the seniors, it was a matter of whether Kelly would be coaching them in the Sugar Bowl. The underclassmen wanted to know who their head coach would be next year.

The answers came on Thursday, December 10, the day of the Bearcats' football banquet at the Westin Hotel in downtown Cincinnati, when the news leaked out on national media that Kelly was leaving for Notre Dame. Frey heard the news on the car radio as he drove to the Westin with his parents for what he thought would be a celebration of the regular season that had just ended.

But there was very little celebration at the banquet. It was all about Kelly, who arrived at about 5:45 and strolled through the lobby flanked by two Cincinnati police officers.

"No word," he said to reporters who tried to question him about reports that he had accepted the Notre Dame job. "We're here to celebrate our seniors."

After the banquet, Kelly met privately with the players and told them that he was leaving, even though they had already heard the news.

"We were probably in there one or two minutes max," Pike said. "He said, 'I appreciate what you guys have done. I appreciate how you helped me get to where I'm going.' Other than that, there were no individual goodbyes. That was it and he was gone."

Several players walked out of the room before Kelly was finished talking and found an assemblage of reporters eager to let them vent.

"I didn't want to hear it," Gilyard told reporters. "I'm fairly disgusted with the situation -- him letting it last this long. Everybody and his mama knew what was going on. I feel like he did our team an injustice. Hopefully he'll pack his things up and get to South Bend in a hurry."

"We don't really care what he has to say anymore," Guidugli said. "He can go talk to his Notre Dame team. We're ready to move forward with whoever wants to move forward with us. He's not on the boat anymore, so we've got to continue on."

"We want to make sure (people) still come out and support us," Daniels said, "because we were the ones out there playing every day, every snap. He was just the one calling the plays."

Not all the players ripped Kelly. Revels and Brad Jones both said they understood his decision and harbored no ill feelings towards him. But overall a thick cloud of anger and bitterness hung over the entire evening.

Kelly couldn't help but feel it.

"Mardy wouldn't even come near me," Kelly said. "He gave me a look. None of the guys were happy because it broke during the banquet. It was the worst banquet I've ever been to. It was pretty close to mutiny during the banquet. It was awful. It was terrible. It was the worst thing that I've been a part of, for that to happen. That's why I'm still upset to this day that it wasn't handled the right way."

Kelly insists that he did nothing wrong. He said he handled his exit exactly the way he promised he would. It wasn't his fault that his decision had hit the news before he had a chance to inform his players in person.

"I did it with integrity and honesty, and it was not handled (properly) by whoever leaked it out to the media," Kelly said. "I think that was unfair to our players to have that happen to them because I always told them, 'You'll be the first to know,' so they should have been mad, they should have been upset because if I was them, I would be too, because that's what I told them. I never lied to them and I never told them something that wasn't true. There was nothing that I could have done differently because I handled it the way it should have been handled."

One of the reasons some of the Cincinnati players were so angry is that they believed Kelly had lied to them. Both Pike and Gilyard had personally asked Kelly when the Notre Dame rumors were beginning to swirl if they were true.

"I remember going to a practice at Nippert Stadium and asking Brian Kelly, there's a lot of rumors going on about you and Notre Dame," Pike said. "I had my arm around him on the sideline and he said, 'Why would I leave Cincinnati? I can play for a national championship here.'

"The reason we had so much success was that everyone on that team bought in together. If a player said something, we bought in. If a coach said something, we bought in. So if Coach Kelly's saying he's going to stay here, then I'm not putting any thought into him not staying here. It turned into there's all these rumors going on, but people don't know what they're talking about. Our coach is our coach and he's going to be here."

Gilyard was more upset about how he felt Kelly handled his departure than he was about Kelly's actual decision to leave for Notre Dame. That part he could understand.

"He handled the whole situation wrong," Gilyard said. "If I had a chance to talk to him today, I'd tell him. He lied to me. He lied to the whole team. I asked him about it personally and he looked at me and said no. So I went in and told the team. But it all turned out to be true."

When Dantonio left for Michigan State in 2006, "he handled it as a professional should," Gilyard said. "He brought all of us in and talked to us. That's how much of a class act Mark Dantonio was. I was so mad at the banquet. (Kelly) said, 'As you guys know, I'm going to Notre Dame.' Are you kidding me? You lied to my face, bro. I remember me walking out. I was just getting rushed by cameras. Could I have handled that situation a little bit different? Yes, but no, I was going to tell it like I felt about it.

"He got credit for winning a lot of games with Mark Dantonio's guys. We would have won regardless, because we had Dantonio's boys there. Mark Dantonio had planted those seeds."

Craig Carey understands the anger many of his teammates felt, but he also believes that some of them misunderstood what Kelly was telling them about the Notre Dame rumors.

"He was very good with the way he worded certain things," Carey said, "so I could definitely understand why players thought he told us that he was going to stay. But I didn't ever take it that way. I loved him. I think he did wonders for the program while we were there and then he took the job of a lifetime. He didn't say he wasn't leaving. He said, 'Right now this is what I'm focused on. I'm here. I'm staying here right now.'"

There's a common belief among Cincinnati fans, many of whom still haven't forgiven Kelly for the way he left, that he was looking to leave Cincinnati from the moment he was hired in

December 2006. When the Notre Dame job opened, they believe, it was a lock that Kelly would jump at the chance to leave the Bearcats. After all, wasn't he looking to leave anyway?

Kelly was definitely ambitious. But it's also true that while he was at Cincinnati he worked tirelessly to promote the program. And he insisted on a new practice facility to enable the Bearcats to work out indoors during inclement weather in late fall. Would a coach who was looking to leave from the moment he arrived had bothered to do either?

"There was no intention of me taking another job," Kelly said. "I didn't come into the season and go through the season with an eye toward, 'Hey, we're winning games, I'm going to get out of here.' My wife was going through cancer. She loves where she lives. We've already been through this at Central Michigan. You want to talk about ultimate pressure on a coach? It's when your wife comes home and says you'd better win because I need to get out of here. That's pressure on a coach. When she comes home and she loves where she is and she loves the people around her, you're not going, 'Where's the next job?' So yeah, I may have said I'm not going anywhere."

Kelly said he didn't consider Notre Dame to be his dream job, but merely the next step in his career, a chance to coach at the most historic program in college football. What coach wouldn't consider leaving his current job for that opportunity?

"There's nothing like it from that perspective," he said. "It had to be Cincinnati to Notre Dame. Cincinnati to anything else, other than the elite of college football, wouldn't have been enough. We were in (the equivalent of) a power five conference. If it is what it is today (the Bearcats are a member of the American Athletic Conference) and it's not a power five conference, it's a different conversation. But we're sitting there and we're going to BCS bowl games in back-to-back years. I'm going to get paid pretty good. I love the city. My wife loves the city. It's a good gig, you know? We're getting our (practice) facility built. We've got a good thing going.

"We were building this thing to sustain it for a long period of time. It wasn't just, 'Let's go.' The vision for it was a sustainable football program playing for championships year after year. What happened after that was the most historic football program got in the way of all that, from my perspective, not Cincinnati's.

"It wasn't my dream job. I didn't ever sit down and dream of an ascension to Notre Dame. I started coaching because I love the relationships. It wasn't, 'Hey, Notre Dame is where I want to end up.' What drew me to Notre Dame and why it ultimately became the dream job is because it became one where it brought all of that together. And then add the ability to have a national presence and the kind of players that allow you those great relationships."

If it weren't for the one second that was put back on the clock in the Texas-Nebraska game, Kelly would have stayed at Cincinnati at least long enough to coach the Bearcats in the national championship game against Alabama.

"You don't come into this profession to not coach in the national championship game," he said. "(Notre Dame) wouldn't

187

have had a choice. They might have moved on, but there's no way in heck am I am giving up an opportunity to play in the national championship game."

Who knows? Perhaps Notre Dame would have refused to wait for Kelly and moved on to someone else. If so, there's a chance that Kelly would have stayed at Cincinnati. But it's hard to imagine that he would still be there 10 years later, after the Big East Conference fell apart and the Bearcats moved to the AAC.

Even without the national championship possibility, Kelly said he considered staying to coach the Bearcats against Florida in the Sugar Bowl, but he concluded that it just wouldn't work.

"It became impossible because of the way it was handled at the end," Kelly said. "The trust was gone. They would not play for me at that point, which was a shame because the outcome could have been different. But that ship had sailed once that leaked out."

17

The Sugar Bowl

Kelly was gone, but the season wasn't over. The Bearcats wouldn't get to play for the national championship and they would have to move forward without their head coach, but they still had the chance to play Florida in the Sugar Bowl. They had about three weeks to gather themselves to face a team that many considered to be the most talented in the country, even though the Gators had lost to Alabama in the SEC championship game.

With Kelly now in South Bend, his coaching staff remained in Cincinnati to prepare the Bearcats for the Sugar Bowl. After their lackluster performance against Virginia Tech in the Orange Bowl the year before, they were determined to make a better showing in their second straight BCS bowl appearance.

To accomplish that goal, it was imperative that they forget about any lingering disappointment about not getting to play for the national championship and concentrate on the task at hand, which was formidable enough in its own right.

"Anybody who knows anything about college football knows that the Florida Gators were one of the best teams in the land," Revels said, "if not *the* best team in the land. They were coming off their national championship. If you run through their roster of who was on that Florida team with Tim Tebow and Riley Cooper and Carlos Dunlap, the Pouncey brothers, Joe Haden…The list goes on and on. Aaron Hernandez was on that team. They had name recognition. Urban Meyer was their coach. If you're overlooking a team like that because of one second for the national championship, you're a fool."

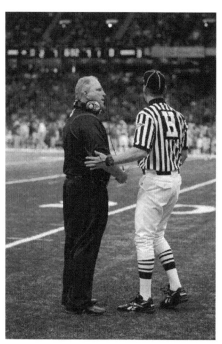

Interim head coach Jeff Quinn coached the Bearcats in the Sugar Bowl after Brian Kelly left for Notre Dame.

In Kelly's absence, offensive coordinator Jeff Quinn was installed as the interim head coach. Given all that had transpired in the past week, it was an almost impossible situation for any coach. Many of the players were still angry about Kelly's departure. Now they had to deal with the defending national champions, who had won two of the past three BCS championships, featuring 2007 Heisman Trophy winner Tebow, and coached by Meyer, who was widely considered the best coach in the country.

As if that wasn't enough to deal with, the Cincinnati assistant coaches who had worked so well together during the season were now faced with the prospect of finding new jobs in a hurry.

"It was a little weird," Kelce said.

The day after Kelly resigned, Thomas met with the assistant coaches and explained that according to their contracts their employment at Cincinnati was tied to Kelly. With Kelly gone, they had 60 days to find new jobs. He told them he would recommend that the new head coach interview all of them for his staff, but the coaches were savvy enough to know that new head coaches like to bring in their own people.

"These guys' world was turned upside down and they're 12-0," Coombs said. "It's not like they were 0-12 and losing their jobs. There was a lot of anxiety about that. Everybody was trying to take care of their own individual house, and then you have to try to figure out how to beat Florida. There wasn't a practice bubble at the time. We practiced outside. The snow was miserable leading up to the game."

Coombs had already been approached by Thomas and deputy AD Bob Arkeilpane and was offered a contract for the following season, which he agreed to. But his colleagues weren't operating under the same level of job security.

"I know how the coaches were feeling," Coombs said. "They were miserable."

A few weeks later, Quinn's job status had been clarified. He likely could have gone to Notre Dame with Kelly, but instead landed his first job as a head coach when Buffalo hired him on December 20 to replace Turner Gill, who had left to become the head coach at Kansas.

But before leaving for Buffalo, Quinn wanted to do right by the Cincinnati players. He felt they deserved that much from him and the rest of the coaching staff and was determined to do all he could to prepare them for Florida.

"When Brian called me," Quinn said, "I was out on the road recruiting for those first couple of days before the banquet. He said, 'Jeff, I need you to do me a favor. I just got offered the Notre Dame job and I'm going to take it. I need you to be the interim head coach. I need you to keep things together and get that team ready. You're going to have that entire coaching staff except myself.'"

Quinn's first decision was to give the players some time off to let them get away from the game and the hard feelings. He urged them to appreciate everything Kelly had done and all the work they had done. Then he reminded them that they still had unfinished business.

Initially Quinn was considered a candidate to replace Kelly on a permanent basis and was interviewed for the job by Thomas and Arkeilpane, but he could tell during the interview that they preferred to hire someone from outside the program. At that point, Quinn said, his entire focus was on doing his best for the players while at the same time defending his friend Kelly.

"I asked them, given the circumstances, 'If it was you, what would you do if you had the chance to go Notre Dame?'" Quinn said. "You'd probably take it just like anybody else would. Let's get back to work. Let's get back and do what we intended to do. Let's complete the mission."

On the surface, things appeared normal to Quinn, but that might have been wishful thinking. The players were still showing up on time for practice, although there wasn't much to those early bowl practices, so there wasn't a lot of intensity required. Meanwhile Quinn stayed in touch with Kelly.

"I had conversations with Brian throughout those two weeks," Quinn said, "and I had great coaches. These guys wanted to win the damn game too. And they wanted their players to perform at the highest level. They were going to be on national television on January 1. I wanted them to be college football players and be the champions that they were, to prepare well, so that they were ready to compete against Florida."

But Binns said there was a lack of focus in preparation among both the players and the coaches. Now that he's the outside receivers coach at Hampton University after a brief NFL career, Binns said he has a better grasp of what was going on with the coaches now as he looks back on it from the perspective of a coach.

"Now that I'm in the profession, I understand what goes on," Binns said. "When a head coach starts to leave, he's going to take some of the guys with him, so they may be coaching, but they know they're only going to be (at that school) for another couple of weeks.

"Then you've got your other pool of guys who don't know if he's taking them and they're contract is up at the end of the year and they might not even have a job. Their minds are all over the place. Our minds are less focused on football and more focused on 'Hey, we're going to New Orleans, let's go have fun and enjoy ourselves.'

This is What the Top Feels Like

Alex Daniels and Ricardo Mathews at the players' Redfish Grill team dinner in New Orleans.

We're undefeated. We're not realizing what's up against us and that's Urban Meyer and that's Tim Tebow in his last game. That's kind of what we were setting ourselves up for."

On December 16, Cincinnati hired Central Michigan head coach Butch Jones to replace Kelly. Jones had replaced Kelly at CMU when Kelly took the Cincinnati job in 2006. He was in New Orleans to watch his new team play in the Sugar Bowl. He stayed in the same hotel as the team did, but for the most part kept a low profile.

The Bearcats left for New Orleans on December 26. They practiced at Tulane University and said all the right things during their media sessions leading up to the Sugar Bowl. Behind the scenes, though, the threads were beginning to unravel.

"It was New Orleans, there was definitely partying going on," Guidugli said. "The confidence or whatever we had for those 12 regular-season games didn't seem to be there during the week. It just

194

wasn't there. So there's probably something to that as far as partying in New Orleans. It was like these coaches won't be our coaches next year, so let's just have good time.

"It all started immediately after the banquet, the whole kind of sour mood and losing the momentum we had. Some guys still wanted to play. Some guys were feeling like somebody jumped ship on us at the most inopportune time. Guys were choosing sides, who's mad at him and who's not? All those things are distractions we weren't dealing with for 12 games. I remember being disappointed and frustrated. It was the fact that he was leaving us high and dry."

One person close to the team, who asked not to be identified, described the situation in New Orleans as "chaos."

"I don't know if they were bitter about Kelly leaving or the way it all went down," he said. "Florida supposedly had some pictures of our guys on Bourbon Street. We had a number of situations, but it was stuff that we were able to keep under control. Players were blaming coaches and coaches were blaming players. It wasn't the most disciplined time for our team."

One night, he said, there was a "physical encounter on the team floor in the hotel where we were staying. It wasn't just one or two guys."

The entire scenario was bizarre for a team that had accomplished so much during the regular season. The seniors had turned their attention to their NFL prospects, and the underclassmen were wondering who would coach them for the rest of their college careers. Basically, it was a mess.

Bearcat players unwind at Rock 'N Bowl in New Orleans.

"It was like Mom left the house for the night," Pead said, "and now all of us children are in the house with no rules. We can do what we want. And it showed. It showed in that game, which was an embarrassment. To be brutally honest, the leadership went right out the door. It was boys being boys. The assistant coaches, it's not that they didn't have authority, but it just wasn't as strong as Kelly's."

The Gators also had a reason to be disappointed when they arrived in New Orleans. After winning the national championship in 2008, with a roster as talented as theirs, they had every reason to expect a second straight title, especially after they won their first 12 games. But unlike the Bearcats, who were at the mercy of Texas, Nebraska and the officials in the Big 12 title game, the Gators had no one to blame but themselves.

How talented was the 2009 Florida team? The Gators had a school-record nine players taken in the 2010 draft, the most of any school in the country. They had six players taken in the first two rounds, including two in the first round -- Tebow and Haden.

They also had their own coach's controversy to deal with. On December 26, Meyer announced that he planned to retire after the Sugar Bowl for health reasons. He had been admitted to a hospital because of chest pains following the SEC championship game. The next day, he changed his retirement to an "indefinite leave of absence" and he was back in time for the start of spring practice. In addition, Tebow, who's still considered one of the greatest college players of all time, was preparing for his final college game. Those were the dominant story lines as the week unfolded.

The Bearcats couldn't match the Gators' star power. If Kelly had been there, he could have gone toe-to-toe with Meyer and Tebow from a charisma standpoint, but Quinn had no such panache. He had little experience dealing with the media.

There's no doubt the Bearcats badly wanted to win the game to show they belonged on the same stage with the nation's best teams. But without Kelly to prepare them, and with the overall disparity in talent, they had no realistic chance to pull an upset, even without the "boys will be boys" approach they had succumbed to.

Florida was ranked third nationally in scoring defense (allowing 11.5 points per game), second in pass defense (150.5), and fourth in total defense (252.8) under defensive coordinator Charlie Strong, who had just been hired to become the head coach at

This is What the Top Feels Like

Louisville.

"They had a tremendous team," Kelce said. "It would have been hard for us with the guys they had no matter what. But when you're in it with your buddies and your guys, you're confident. We thought we were one of the best teams in the country at that point. Unfortunately, we didn't get to put our best foot forward. But looking back on it now, with the caliber of players they had versus where we were at, everything was going to have to go right for us to win that one."

Nonetheless, Tebow was complimentary of the Bearcats leading up to the game.

"I had an opportunity during the year to watch a couple of their games," he said. "Obviously, they've had a lot of turmoil with their coaches, with two of them taking head coaching jobs. They're going through a pretty big whirlwind just like we are. You kind of understand where they're coming from."

Equipment manager Barry Boyd gets the Bearcats' new white helmets ready for the Sugar Bowl.

The Bearcats had a sartorial surprise for their fans and the national television audience when they took the field at the Superdome. They came out for their pre-game warm-ups wearing their customary black helmets. But when they came back out for the start of the game, they were decked out in gleaming, new white helmets to match their white uniforms.

Mike Waddell, Senior Associate Director of Athletics for External Relations, took great pains to keep the white helmets a secret because he wanted to make a big splash with them on national TV. I remember seeing one after a practice session that week. When I asked about the helmet, I was told they were top secret and off the record. It seemed an odd thing to be concerned with,

The Bearcats take the field to face Florida sporting their new helmets.

given all that had transpired since the Pitt game had ended. I mentioned the helmets briefly in the notes package I wrote for the Enquirer the next day. Indeed, they did make for a nice visual impact when the players took the field just before the start of the game, but once the game started, they were quickly forgotten.

Tebow saved his best game for his last in a 51-24 rout of the Bearcats, completing 31 of 35 passes for a career-high 482 yards, which was both a Sugar Bowl and a BCS bowl record. The Gators, who were 13-1 entering the game, gained 659 yards in total offense, the most in Sugar Bowl history.

This is What the Top Feels Like

The Bearcats had the ball first, starting at their 27-yard line after Gilyard's 20-yard kickoff return. Pike threw for six yards to Gilyard and for 10 yards to Guidugli. After a personal foul against

Tim Tebow ended his illustrious Florida career in grand fashion by passing for a Sugar Bowl record 482 yards.

Florida, Cincinnati had first-and-10 at the Florida 42. Ramsey then ran 13 yards to the Florida 29, but the play was called back because of a holding call against Chris Jurek, which set up first-and-20 from the Cincinnati 48. On fourth-and-17, Rogers punted 33 yards to the Florida 16.

It took the Gators 13 plays to go 84 yards for a touchdown on Tebow's seven-yard pass to Hernandez, but the extra-point was no good. After the Bearcats went three-and-out, Florida drove 58 yards in eight plays to set up Caleb Sturgis for a 40-yard field goal. By the end of the first quarter, Florida had outgained Cincinnati 124 yards to 30 and Tebow had thrown for 124 yards, completing all 10 of his passes.

But the Bearcats trailed by only nine points and were still in the game, even if the statistics were heavily weighted in Florida's favor. By the end of the first half, though, Florida held a 30-3 lead and Tebow had passed for 320 yards, a Sugar Bowl record for a half. He had completed his first 12 passes.

"At the beginning of the game, it felt a little normal," Webster said. "Guys were wound up and ready to go. But I remember coming in at halftime and seeing guys almost checked out. Guys were just zoned out. The normal things we used to do at halftime when Coach Kelly was there, it wasn't the same. You had Coach Quinn come in and he said a little bit, but he didn't say much. There wasn't any togetherness. There was just no direction. It was very vanilla, especially with play calling. We didn't feel like there was any surprise to what we were running on defense."

The situation was no better on offense.

Jeff Quinn's offense had a difficult time against Florida's elite defense.

"It's a lot harder to game-plan when you can't call the plays with the level of quickness that we were used to," Pike said. "That was the biggest difference early on in that game. Our chance of winning that game would have been tempo and how fast we played. With what Florida was able to do defensively, we just weren't able to get in the tempo and get the plays called fast enough.

"You're asking Jeff Quinn to come in and call the plays when he hadn't done it all year against the best defense in the country. I looked over at him and he was looking over the play sheet and flipping it over. Brian Kelly's best feature was calling the offense. That's where he was a genius.

"I had confidence in the weapons we had if we could push tempo and keep them off balance a little bit. I still felt going in that they hadn't seen an offense like ours. But when the tempo wasn't working, it was going to be a tall task. In college football, you're used to playing against one, two, maybe three guys on defense that are NFL caliber. Half of their defense played in the NFL."

Pike knew before any of his teammates what the Bearcats would be up against when they played Florida. He dissected the game film as any quarterback would, and saw how talented the Gators were. He understood that they would be unlike any opponent they had faced in the past two years, maybe the best Cincinnati had ever faced.

The Bearcats managed 55 yards of offense in the first half They were so overmatched that at halftime Diaco asked Quinn to use as much of the play clock as he could in the second half and to call more running plays to keep the clock moving.

"It was ridiculous," Frey said. "They were running a really high-profile offense and they were prepared for the game. I just felt like we were on our heels the whole game. Offensively, we had some spurts here and there, but once you get behind by three scores, we were lacking the resiliency that we had really relied upon throughout the season."

The Bearcats did manage to score 24 points against Florida, the second-most that any of its opponents had scored all season behind only the 32 that Alabama put up in the SEC championship game. But Cincinnati gained only 246 total yards, by far its lowest total of the season. Pike finished with 27 completions in 45 attempts for 170 yards and three touchdown passes, to Binns, Marcus Waugh and Alli. Pead gained 48 yards on seven carries. Gilyard caught seven passes for 41 yards. Binns and Guidugli each had five receptions. Woods had four.

It was a sound beating, a terrible way to end the greatest season in Cincinnati football history. And it left a sour taste in the mouths of the Cincinnati players as they walked off the Superdome field, many of them for the last time in a Cincinnati uniform.

"We were losing, 30-3, at halftime, but I thought we were going to come back," Pead said. "For reality to hit, it was a learning experience for me, that you're not invincible. Nobody's invincible, and it started with the leadership leaving. The discipline wasn't there. No matter how focused I was or how good I was, we lost as a team. We weren't locked in. I just started crying. I knew the locker room wasn't going to be the same and the feeling wasn't going to be the same. It was like being hit in the stomach. I still say we went 12-0 that season. I don't even count that game."

Coombs acknowledges that the Bearcats, who finished 12-1, lacked the leadership to compete with a team of Florida's caliber. And he says he could have done a better job of getting the players prepared.

"Having said all that," Coombs said, "even if everything was perfect and we were preparing at the highest level, there was certainly no guarantee that we were going to win that game. We were going to be more competitive if Brian was there, but even if we did everything right, that wasn't Pittsburgh we were playing. They were real."

After the game Quinn told his players they should be proud of what they had accomplished.

"I told them I knew it didn't go the way they wanted it to (against Florida)," he said. "It was a tough loss. I told them, 'The best thing you can do is find a way to enjoy an unbelievable season and what you guys did together. That will always be there for you.'"

Kelly started to watch the game on television, but he turned it off at halftime.

"It wasn't the same team," he said. "I could tell it wasn't the same team."

Would the outcome have been different if Kelly had coached the Bearcats? Perhaps, but no one who faced that powerful Florida team that day is bold enough to say the Bearcats would have beaten the Gators, only that the score would have been closer.

"It would have been competitive," Kelly said.

When it was over, Diaco, assistant head coach Mike Elston, running backs coach Tim Hinton, strength coach Paul Longo and passing game coordinator Charley Molnar all joined Kelly on his first staff at Notre Dame. Quarterbacks coach Greg Forest, outside linebackers coach William Inge and director of player services Ernest Jones all accompanied Quinn to Buffalo. Trainer Bob Mangine, assistant AD for football operations John Widecan, video coordinator John Sells and recruiting assistant Gerry Beauchamp all stayed at Cincinnati to work under Jones.

The players left New Orleans with a hollow feeling. As time went by, some of them began to feel as if what they accomplished that season was overshadowed by Kelly's departure and the lopsided loss in the Sugar Bowl.

"We didn't get our gifts at the senior banquet," Pike said. "I was so upset and frustrated about what happened. It should have been celebrating the best season in UC football history, being ranked No. 3 in the country. It should have been a lot more than it was."

18

Hall of Fame

On May 6, 2019, Cincinnati announced that the entire 2009 football team would be inducted into the James P. Kelly Hall of Fame, including Brian Kelly, who agreed to return to Nippert Stadium on Saturday, October 19, when the team will be recognized during the Cincinnati-Tulsa game.

When the announcement was made that Kelly would be inducted, many Cincinnati fans, still angry over the way he left for Notre Dame, protested on talk radio and social media, the scars from his sudden departure apparently still not healed.

But most of the players, some of whom were the most outspoken at the banquet that night back in 2009, have long since gotten over any hard feelings they had for their former coach.

When I asked Guidugli, one of the players who ripped Kelly to reporters that night, what he would say to Kelly now, he said, "I would give him a hug. I have nothing but good things to say about him. There are no hard feelings on my part. It was just a major downer. It was such a great year to have things go that way (at the end). It was just a very odd way to end such a successful year."

Most of the other players I talked to feel the same way about Kelly:

John Goebel: "Brian Kelly leaving is something that I still think about to this day. I don't hold it against him. I'm just glad I got to be a part of it."

Armon Binns: "Your initial thought was anger because you would have liked the information to come a little bit differently, but as you grow older, you understand life, you understand business, especially with me going through the NFL. You start to focus more on things you appreciated. I appreciated him giving me a chance to play at the university. I appreciate the time and effort they put into coaching and teaching us, and how much fun we had. You don't forget all those great moments just because it didn't end the way you want."

Aaron Webster: "I felt for the guys he recruited. I felt for the guys that he told he was going to be here for years. But at the end of the day, we all knew what we signed up for. College football is a business. (The coaches) get an opportunity to better their lives and their family's lives. I can't fault any man for doing that. How he went about it, I would have done it different if I was him. But 10 years later, I have no animosity toward the man. He's doing a wonderful job at Notre Dame."

Drew Frey: "It was the most awkward time. When Butch (Jones) left my senior year, he called us at seven in the morning and told us he was leaving. It wasn't like the radio told everyone before he told us. That's why a lot of people in Cincinnati didn't like Brian Kelly for a while. Or maybe they still don't. I don't know."

Andre Revels: "I wasn't mad at the time and I'm still not

mad today. I compliment BK and his ability to climb the charts. There was never any animosity from me, but I know some of the players felt slighted. College football, when you hit that level, and also the pros, it's a business. And for him to get his dream job at Notre Dame with his background, I have nothing but positive things to say about Brian Kelly and his tenure at Cincinnati and also at Notre Dame."

Tony Pike: "At the time, I didn't like the way he handled it because I had been a part of it with Mark Dantonio coming in after the Rutgers game and saying, 'Hey, I want to be transparent with you guys. I'm going to Michigan State to interview for this job. It's been a dream job of mine.' I felt that was the way to handle stuff. Sitting here ten years later, it's one of those situations where what's happened. I'm more at this point thankful that he spent time at UC and helped me, helped my career, and for the two seasons that we were able to have."

Brad Jones: "I felt a little bit disappointed that we were undefeated and losing our head coach before going to a BCS bowl game, but at the same time you've got to understand that's a once-in-a-lifetime job. You wouldn't criticize any teammate who decided to leave a year early to play at the next level. As a 22-year-old you really don't get it, but as I've grown and matured I totally understand it."

Jason Kelce: "As a college student, you have a loyalty to your program. You haven't really been exposed to the business side of it. It's hard to fathom why someone would leave. Now, looking back, you understand. They've got to make decisions based on the best interest of their family.

"At the time, we were going to a big-time bowl game, it was a pretty big hit to the entire team, to say the least. The reality is what he did at Cincinnati, not just for my career, but for all of our careers and the success we had there, that's a credit to him and the staff that he put together. I've got nothing but positive things to say about that guy. Everybody was upset when he decided to leave. Maybe he could have done it a little better way, but that's all water under the bridge at this point. I don't hold any grudges against him."

Alex Daniels regrets what he said publicly about Brian Kelly when Kelly left for Notre Dame.

The player who expressed the most appreciation for what Kelly did at Cincinnati was Daniels, who was among the most outspoken in his criticism of Kelly at the banquet in 2009.

"I cussed him out on TV because that's how I felt at the time," Daniels said, "but I owe that man an apology because that man saved my life. When we come back (for the Hall of Fame), I'm going to cry and give him the biggest hug ever and tell him I'm sorry for saying bad about him. I never should have because I knew what me and him had. Our relationship was totally different than everybody else's. I knew that was his dream job at Notre Dame. I should have given him all of the applause because he gave me the opportunity to play football again. That's my love and I love that man for that.

"He was the only person to give me a chance to play college football again. For me to say anything bad about that man would be a smack in his face, and I would never do it again. Coach Kelly is the best coach I've ever had still to this day. Period. Point blank. He could recruit and he could bring the best out of any player. He was a winner. He didn't talk about nothing but winning. We went from being the worst laughingstock in college football to being at the top of the totem pole.

"It was the best time of my life. We changed the demographic of the program. I would give my left pinky toe to go back and play another game in that year, just to go back and put that jersey and helmet on, be in that stadium, standing up, spying the quarterback."

Gilyard, a second-team All-American that year, is the one player who steadfastly refuses to take back what he said about Kelly on that December night in 2009.

"I would say to him, 'Man, you didn't have to lie,'" Gilyard said. "'You should have just told us the truth.'"

After their loss to Florida, the Bearcats fell to No. 8 in the final AP poll, No. 9 in the USA Today coaches' poll. They haven't come close to reaching those heights since.

The following spring, Gilyard was drafted in the fourth round by the St. Louis Rams, Pike in the sixth round by the Carolina Panthers, and Ricardo Mathews in the seventh round by the Indianapolis Colts. Seven more players from the 2009 team -- Jason Kelce, Robinson, John Hughes, Pead, Wolfe, Travis Kelce, and punter Patrick O'Donnell -- were drafted over the next three seasons. Both of the Kelce brothers, Wolfe, and O'Donnell are still playing in the NFL.

Kelly is about to embark on his 11th season at Notre Dame. He has had one losing season during his previous 10 years, in 2016 when the Fighting Irish went 4-8. In 2013, he guided Notre Dame to the BCS championship game, where the Irish lost, 42-14, to Alabama. In 2018, he took them to the College Football Playoff semifinals, where they lost to eventual national champion Clemson, 30-3.

At Notre Dame, Kelly's overall record entering the 2019 season was 81-35, leaving him fifth in school history in victories behind Knute Rockne (105), Lou Holtz (100), Ara Parseghian (95) and Frank Leahy (87).

Cincinnati has had three head coaches since Kelly left. Jones went 24-14 before leaving in 2012 to become the head coach at

Tennessee. Tommy Tuberville was fired after going 29-22 in four seasons. Current head coach Luke Fickell was 15-10 in his first two seasons with the Bearcats.

For some, the 2009 season is remembered primarily for what happened at the end, with Kelly's departure and the lopsided loss to Florida. If so, that's a shame. The players and coaches on that team deserve much better.

"There are stories from that year that I feel even if we tried to describe them in a million words can't showcase the bond that's there," Revels said. "When I think about 2009, it's more about feelings and emotions rather than words that go through me. When people think of our legacy it's the first 12-win season, first perfect regular season that the University of Cincinnati had. That's what our legacy is. For anyone to say that our legacy is defined by our coach leaving before the Sugar Bowl doesn't know the team."

The players I talked to for this book all echoed what Revels said. They talked about the bond that existed -- and still does -- among the players, and about how honored they are to have been a part of it. And even though some of them understand that fans might remember the team for Kelly's abrupt exit and the Sugar Bowl fiasco, they know better.

"I don't think there's any question that the dominant story line for that entire season is that Brian Kelly left," Coombs said. "That would be what everybody remembers about that season. But it was a magical season. It's so unfortunate that's what people remember. If you vilify Brian Kelly, that's a mistake. That's foolish on people's part. The only reason we were there is because of what Brian Kelly did at the University of Cincinnati. The only reason."

How special was that season to the Cincinnati players? Jason Kelce won a Super Bowl at the end of the 2017 season with the Philadelphia Eagles, but to him, what the Bearcats accomplished in 2009 is just as special.

"Quite frankly, what we accomplished that year at Cincinnati might be more impressive than winning the Super Bowl," Kelce said. "The Big East was a big-time conference, but it was much under the Big Ten, the Pac 12, and those other conferences. We weren't getting the same type of recruits that a lot of those other schools were getting.

"Besides (Florida and Alabama), I don't know that there's anybody in college football that we weren't going to be confident against. We were just about as good as anybody outside those two teams. And we did it with a bunch of guys that weren't five-star recruits. We did with a lot of hard-working, blue-collar players and great coaches. That was one of my favorite years playing football of all time. We lost only one game that year and I had a great time playing with some of my best friends still to this day."

Being inducted into Cincinnati's Hall of Fame means a lot to Kelly. He didn't like the way things unfolded at the end either, even if he doesn't believe he did anything wrong.

"I'm not looking for that to heal anything," Kelly said. "It means something to me because of the players. It means something to me because of the respect I have for that group in particular and for the way UC treated me. You don't come back unless you were treated right and you love the players you were with.

"It's hard to say what your greatest accomplishment is, but it's my most satisfying because of the collection of guys on that roster. These guys overcame a lot to put themselves into perfection, if you will. We were able to paint a vision for them and in doing so, create a culture for them that really worked. And that's really satisfying."

Binns still gets asked about the catch that enabled the Bearcats to beat Pittsburgh in the Big East championship game.

"What's crazy to me is how the fans every year show so much love and appreciation for that play and for that season," Binns said. "Every year Twitter goes crazy. Every time I talk to family or friends or just people who know anything about UC football, it's like, 'Oh man, you're the guy who made the catch.' It's cool to be part of that. It's a lot to take in when you think about me being a guy who had one scholarship offer coming out of high school, coming all the way from California and being able to be a part of that ride."

2009 Big East Champions

2009 Cincinnati Football Roster

No.	Name	Pos.	Ht.	Wt.	Cl.	Hometown
8	Kazeem Alli	TE	6-4	258	SR	St. Louis, MO
14	Chazz Anderson	QB	6-0	209	SO	Pickerington, OH
86	Blake Annen	TE	6-4	220	FR	Upper Arlington, OH
51	Alex Apyan	LS	6-2	205	SO	Chattanooga, TN
85	Marcus Barnett	DB	6-2	174	JR	Forestville, MD
69	Frank Becker	OL	6-1	287	SO	Cincinnati, OH
80	Armon Binns	WR	6-4	200	JR	Pasadena, CA
38	Brent Black	DB	6-1	194	SO	Cincinnati, OH
20	Maalik Bomar	LB	6-1	195	FR	Cincinnati, OH
76	Austen Bujnoch	OL	6-5	265	FR	Cincinnati, OH
89	John Canafax	WR	5-11	177	SO	Covington, KY
7	Craig Carey	LB	6-4	248	SR	Cincinnati, OH
21	Camerron Cheatham	DB	5-9	187	FR	Kalamazoo, MI
57	Obadiah Cheatham	LB	6-2	224	JR	Cincinnati, OH
55	Angel Clybourne	LB	6-1	226	FR	Mays Landing, NJ
70	C.J. Cobb	OL	6-4	304	JR	Jacksonville, FL
12	Zach Collaros	QB	6-0	209	SO	Steubenville, OH
42	Austin Cook	LB	6-0	210	JR	Chicago, I
41	Michael Cooke	P	6-2	210	SO	Cincinnati, OH
79	Andre Cureton	OL	6-6	280	FR	Indianapolis, IN
4	Alex Daniels	DL	6-4	259	SR	Columbus, OH
72	Evan Davis	OL	6-4	262	SO	Cincinnati, OH
39	Alex Delisi	LB	6-2	225	SO	Clarkston, MI
67	Adam Dempsey	DL	6-3	252	FR	Fort Thomas, KY
96	Tom DeTemple	LS	6-2	225	SO	Cincinnati, OH
10	Romel Dismuke	DB	5-8	180	FR	Cleveland, OH
65	T.J. Franklin	OL	6-4	287	SO	Maryville, TN
26	Drew Frey	DB	6-4	205	FR	Wilmington, OH
1	Mardy Gilyard	WR	6-1	187	SR	Bunnell, FL
99	Dan Giordano	DL	6-4	246	FR	Frankfort, IL
22	John Goebel	RB	6-1	213	JR	Milford, MI
66	Sam Griffin	OL	6-4	260	JR	Englewood, NJ
19	Ben Guidugli	TE	6-0	237	JR	Fort Thomas, KY
23	Rueben Haley	DB	6-0	188	SO	Cincinnati, OH
59	Steve Hancock	DL	6-3	233	SO	Sterling, VA
44	Rick Harris	DL	6-2	308	FR	Westerville, OH
81	Tomaz Hilton	WR	6-3	215	SO	Youngstown, OH
92	Michael Hilty	DL	6-4	242	FR	Powell, OH
31	Quentin Hines	RB	5-11	185	FR	Detroit, MI
59	Alex Hoffman	OL	6-5	294	SO	Indianapolis, IN
77	Sean Hooey	OL	6-8	296	FR	Litchfield, MI

31	Bruce Horner	DB	5-11	171	FR	Farmington Hills, MI
87	Charley Howard	WR	6-3	205	SR	Gahanna, OH
6	Jamar Howard	WR	6-4	210	JR	Cincinnati, OH
40	John Hughes	DL	6-2	305	SO	Gahanna, OH
18	Malik James	DB	6-1	190	SO	Los Angeles, CA
5	Reuben Johnson	DB	5-10	173	FR	Atco, NJ
46	Scott Johnson	RB	5-10	204	SO	Middletown, OH
25	Brad Jones	DB	6-1	202	SR	Canton, OH
2	Demetrius Jones	LB	6-4	214	JR	Chicago, IL
81	Josh Jones	WR	6-3	210	FR	Cincinnati, OH
56	Chris Jurek	OL	6-2	286	SR	Southfield, MI
11	Brendon Kay	QB	6-4	227	FR	Ira, MI
60	Jason Kelce	OL	6-4	290	JR	Cleveland Heights, OH
18	Travis Kelce	TE	6-5	247	FR	Cleveland Heights, OH
64	Mitch Kessel	OL	6-5	265	FR	Bloomfield Hills, MI
33	Aaron Kingcade	P	6-3	195	FR	Columbus, OH
13	Pat Lambert	DB	6-1	193	FR	St. Cloud, FL
71	Jeff Linkenbach	OL	6-6	311	SR	Sandusky, OH
47	Colin Lozier	LB	6-0	210	FR	Cincinnati, OH
53	Randy Martinez	OL	6-1	277	SO	Teaneck, NJ
90	Ricardo Mathews	DL	6-3	294	SR	Jacksonville, FL
11	Collin McCafferty	LB	6-3	222	JR	Maineville, OH
49	Sean McClellan	DL	6-4	265	FR	Cincinnati, OH
46	Mitch Meador	DL	6-4	240	FR	Greenwood, IN
83	Danny Milligan	WR	5-9	171	FR	Cincinnati, OH
58	Brandon Mills	DL	5-10	266	FR	Cincinnati, OH
34	Patrick O'Donnell	P/K	6-5	210	FR	Wellington, FL
68	Craig Parmenter	OL	6-5	289	SO	Ringwood, NJ
91	Ryan Paxson	DL	6-6	220	FR	Brighton, MI
82	Lynell Payne	WR	6-3	205	FR	Marlton, NJ
23	Isaiah Pead	WR	5-10	193	SO	Columbus, OH
15	Tony Pike	QB	6-6	210	SR	Cincinnati, OH
26	Quincy Quetant	DB	6-1	209	FR	Orlando, FL
41	Jared Rains	DB	5-10	193	FR	Aliquippa, PA
20	Jacob Ramsey	RB	6-0	216	SR	Columbus, OH
50	Andre Revels	LB	6-0	221	SR	Cincinnati, OH
13	Demetrius Richardson	QB	6-3	220	FR	Marlton, NJ
24	Wesley Richardson	DB	6-0	193	SO	Columbus, OH
88	Adrien Robinson	TE	6-4	244	SO	Indianapolis, IN
97	Jake Rogers	K	6-3	205	JR	Warsaw, IN
33	Luca Romeo	TE	6-1	218	FR	Cincinnati, OH
16	Will Saddler	DB	6-4	210	FR	Columbus, IN
37	JK Schaffer	LB	6-1	223	SO	Cincinnati, OH
48	Brady Slusher	LB	6-2	217	FR	Fort Mitchell, KY
63	Dan Sprague	OL	6-3	260	FR	Worthington, OH
94	Jordan Stepp	DL	6-0	286	FR	Asheville, OH

12	Mark Tabar	K	6-2	180	FR	Cincinnnati, OH
10	Monte Taylor	DL	6-5	245	JR	Los Angeles, CA
52	Ricardo Thompson	LB	6-1	227	SO	Cincinnati, OH
45	Rob Trigg	DE	6-3	264	JR	Dayton, OH
35	Marcus Waugh	LB	6-0	270	SR	Whitehouse, OH
17	Aaron Webster	DB	6-2	211	SR	Southfield, MI
19	Chris Williams	DB	6-0	190	FR	Cincinnati, OH
7	Darrin Williams	RB	5-7	180	FR	Detroit, MI
48	Trammell Williams	DB	5-9	185	SO	Cincinnati, OH
93	Mike Windt	LS	6-2	250	SR	Cincinnati, OH
32	George Winn	RB	5-11	202	FR	Southfield, MI
95	Derek Wolfe	DL	6-5	302	SO	Lisbon, OH
3	D.J. Woods	WR	6-0	175	SO	Strongsville, OH
84	Orion Woodard	WR	6-2	214	SO	Pompton Lakes, NJ
98	Curtis Young	DE	6-1	269	SR	Cleveland, OH

COACHING STAFF

Head coach: Brian Kelly; offensive coordinator, offensive line coach: Jeff Quinn; defensive coordinator, inside linebackers: Bob Diaco; associate head coach, defensive backs: Kerry Coombs; assistant coach, special teams coordinator, defensive line: Mike Elston; passing game coordinator, wide receivers: Charley Molnar; recruiting coordinator, running backs: Tim Hinton; quarterbacks: Greg Forest; tight ends, Lorenzo Guess; ourside linebackers: William Inge; director of player services: Ernest Jones.

SUPPORT STAFF

Director of football strength and conditioning: Paul Longo; football athletic trainer: Bob Mangine; assistant AD/football operations: John Widecan; football program associate: Beth Rex; director, division of sports medicine: Angelo Colosimo; head equipment manager: Barry Boyd; video coordinator: John Sells; recruiting assistant: Gerry Beauchamp; graduate assistant: Jon Carpenter; staff associate: Mike Daniels; assistant strength coach: Jacob Flint; staff associate: Mike Painter; graduate assistant: Marty Spieler.

Source:2009 University of Cincinnati football media guide: Ryan Koslen, editor.

Season in Review

Game 1
CINCINNATI 47, RUTGERS 15

Monday, Sept. 7
Attendance: 53,737

Rutgers Stadium
Piscataway, New Jersey

"We came out with a chip on our shoulder knowing that we had a chance on national TV

to show the college football universe what we can do."

-Quarterback Tony Pike

Despite coming off a Big East championship and an appearance in the Orange Bowl, the Bearcats were not ranked in the Associated Press Top 25 to start the season. They made an immediate statement with a 47-15 blowout of Rutgers on the day the Scarlet Knights celebrated the opening of their expanded stadium. Tony Pike completed his first six passes and Cincinnati needed only 2:29 to score its first touchdown. He finished with 22 completions in 34 attempts for 362 yards and three touchdowns with one interception. Mardy Gilyard caught eight passes for 89 yards. Isaiah Pead scored on 41-yard touchdown reception. The Bearcats closed the first half with 24 unanswered points to lead 31-7 at halftime. The following week they checked in at No. 23 in the Associated Press media poll.

Score by quarter	1	2	3	4	FINAL
Cincinnati	7	24	14	2	47
Rutgers	7	0	0	8	15

1st quarter
12:31 - CIN Pead 2 run (Rogers kick)
1:47 - RUT Martinek 4 run (Te kick)

2nd quarter
13:48 - CIN Rogers 30 FG
6:35 - CIN T. Kelce 4 run (Rogers kick)
2:30 - CIN Gilyard 5 pass from Pike (Rogers kick)
0:54 - CIN Pead 41 pass from Pike (Rogers kick)

3rd quarter
7:42 - CIN T. Kelce 2 run (Rogers kick)
1:10 - CIN Ramsey 1 pass from Pike (Rogers kick)

4th quarter
1:25 - RUT Graves 7 pass from Savage (Sanu pass from Savage)
6:59 - CIN Team safety

Cincinnati stats
RUSHING LEADERS: Ramsey 8-77-0, Pead 8-47-1
PASSING LEADERS: Pike 27-34-362-1 3 TD, Collaros 2-2-34-0 0 TD
RECEIVING LEADERS: Gilyard 8-89-1, Binns 5-41-0, Woods 4-71-0
TACKLING LEADERS: Young 11, Webster 10, B. Jones 7, D. Jones 7, Revels 7, Daniels 7
INTERCEPTIONS: Webster 1, D. Jones 1, Schaffer 1

Rutgers stats
RUSHING LEADERS: Martinek 15-54-1
PASSING LEADERS: Savage 15-23-135-0 1 TD, Natale 8-12-108-3 0 TD
RECEIVING LEADERS: Sanu 10-101-0, Brown 7-86-0
TACKLING LEADERS: Lefeged 9, D'Imperio 8, Lowery 6, McCourty 6
INTERCEPTIONS: Silvestro 1

Records: Cincinnati 1-0, Rutgers 0-1

Game 2
No. 23 CINCINNATI 70, SOUTHEAST MISSOURI STATE 3

Saturday, Sept. 12
Attendance: 30,421

Nippert Stadium
Cincinnati, Ohio

"This team is a special team."

- Wide receiver Mardy Gilyard

Cincinnati scored seven touchdowns in the first half, starting with a 53-yard punt return by Mardy Gilyard 2:09 into the game and led, 49-3, at halftime. The Bearcats gained 578 yards to 176 for SE Missouri State, a school from the lower- level Football Championship Subdivision. The 67-point margin of victory was the largest for Cincinnati since a 67-0 victory over Virginia Military Institute in 1953. Cincinnati redshirt freshman Darrin Williams returned the second-half kickoff 100 yards for a touchdown. Aaron Webster, Dominique Battle and Andre Revels each intercepted a pass. Gilyard scored four touchdowns on a punt return, a one-yard run, an eight-yard pass and a 37-yard pass.

Score by quarter	1	2	3	4	FINAL
SE Missouri St.	3	0	0	0	3
Cincinnati	21	28	14	7	70

1st quarter
12:51 - CIN Gilyard 53 punt return (Rogers kick)
5:55 - SEMO Spada 23 FG
3:44 - CIN Ramsey 19 pass from Pike (Rogers kick)
2:15 - CIN Pike 1 run (Rogers kick)

2nd quarter
14:23 - CIN Gilyard 1 run (Rogers kick)
10:38 - CIN Gilyard 8 pass from Pike (Rogers kick)
4:41 - CIN Barnett 14 pass from Pike (Rogers kick)
1:32 - CIN Gilyard 37 pass from Collaros (Rogers kick)

3rd quarter
14:48 - CIN D. Williams 100 kickoff return (Rogers kick)
9:17- CIN Howard 43 pass from Collaros (Rogers kick)

4th quarter
8:04 - CIN Johnson 33 run (Rogers kick)

SE Missouri St. stats
RUSHING LEADERS: Harris 10-42-0, Jones 11-29-0
PASSING LEADERS: Scheible 15-27-123-3 0 TD
RECEIVING LEADERS: Peoples 4-38-0, Edwards 3-34-0,
Ahamefule 3-26-0, Stewart 3-15-0
TACKLING LEADERS: Jackson 7, Calvin 7, Anderson 7
INTERCEPTIONS: 0

Cincinnati stats
RUSHING LEADERS: Ramsey 7-65-0, Pead 11-45-0, Johnson 2-35-1
PASSING LEADERS: Pike 17-23-229-0 3 TD, Collaros 4-9-95-0 2 TD
RECEIVING LEADERS: Gilyard 6-111-2, Binns 4-77-0, Barnett 3-35-1,
Woods 3-20-0
TACKLING LEADERS: Mills 7, Armstrong 6, Trigg 6, Battle 5
INTERCEPTIONS: Battle 1, Revels 1, Webster 1

Records: Cincinnati 2-0, SE Missouri St. 1-1

Game 3
No. 17 CINCINNATI 28, OREGON STATE 18

Saturday, Sept. 19   Reser Stadium
Attendance: 41,909   Corvallis, Oregon

"We've won two games now on the road early in the season. I think that tells you

a little bit about what kind of football team we have."

- Head coach Brian Kelly

Cincinnati ended Oregon State's 26-game winning streak in non-conference home games, a streak that dated to 1996. The Bearcats' offense was shut down in the first quarter, failing to record a first down until the 1:41 mark of the period and trailed 6-0 at the end of the period, but scored 21 points in the second quarter to lead, 21-8, at halftime. OSU pulled within six at 21-15 early in the third quarter, then picked off a Tony Pike pass and returned it to its own 46-yard line, but was forced to punt. After a short punt, the Beavers drove to the Cincinnati five-yard line where they had first-and-goal, but settled for a six-yard field goal. A 19-yard touchdown pass from Pike to Mardy Gilyard gave Cincinnati a 28-18 lead with 8:03 remaining. UC wide receiver D.J. Woods caught seven passes for 117 yards, both career highs, and had his first career touchdown reception, a 45-yard pass from Pike.

Score by quarter	1	2	3	4	FINAL
Cincinnati	0	21	0	7	28
Oregon State	6	2	7	3	18

1st quarter
12:13 - OSU Kahut 46 FG
6:11 - OSU Kahut 39 FG

2nd quarter
14:27 - CIN Pike 7 run (Rogers kick)
12:13 - OSU Team safety
6:40 - CIN Pead 1 run (Rogers kick)
0:18 - CIN Woods 45 pass from Pike (Rogers kick)

3rd quarter
12:36 - OSU Jacq. Rodgers 9 run (Kahut kick)

4th quarter
13:22 - OSU Kahut 23 FG
8:03 - CIN Gilyard 19 pass from Pike (Rogers kick)

Cincinnati stats
RUSHING LEADERS: Pead 11-46-1, Ramsey 5-19-0, Pike 6-15-1
PASSING LEADERS: Pike 31-49-332-1 2 TD
RECEIVING LEADERS: Gilyard 9-65-1, Woods 7-117-1, Binns 6-61-0
TACKLING LEADERS: Frey 12, Revels 9, Schaffer 8
INTERCEPTIONS: Schaffer 1

Oregon State stats
RUSHING LEADERS: Jacq. Rodgers 20-73-1, James Rodgers 11-67-0
PASSING LEADERS: Canfield 29-45-240-1 0 TD
RECEIVING LEADERS: James Rodgers 11-90-0, Adeniji 5-57-0,
Jacq. Rodgers 5-19-0
TACKLING LEADERS: Collins 8, Kristick 8, Pa'aluhi 7, Roberson 7
INTERCEPTIONS: Kristick 1

Records: Cincinnati 3-0, Oregon State 2-1

Game 4
No. 14 CINCINNATI 28, FRESNO STATE 20

Saturday, Sept. 26   Nippert Stadium
Attendance: 32,910   Cincinnati, Ohio

"He's big, strong, fast, and had real strong feet. I'm just glad we got through it."

- Linebacker JK Schaffer on Ryan Mathews

Fresno State entered the game determined to use its formidable running attack to keep Cincinnati's high-powered offense off the field as much as possible. And it almost worked. The Bulldogs had the ball on offense for 43 minutes, 42 seconds, compared with 16 minutes, 18 seconds for the Bearcats. Fresno State running back Ryan Mathews gained 145 yards on 38 carries. Cincinnati was clinging to a 21-17 lead early in the fourth quarter when the Bulldogs faced a fourth-and-two at the Cincinnati six-yard line. Instead of giving the ball to Mathews, quarterback Ryan Colburn attempted a pass that was intercepted by linebacker Craig Carey, who returned it 21 yards to the Cincinnati 29. Six plays later, Tony Pike completed a 23-yard touchdown pass to Mardy Gilyard with 13:09 to play. Jake Rogers' extra point kick made it 28-20. The Bulldogs took possession on their own eight for their final drive and drove to the Cincinnati 38, but their drive stalled with an incomplete pass on fourth and eight with 39 seconds left. Gilyard had nine catches for 177 yards and two touchdowns, giving him eight touchdown passes in four games.

Score by quarter	1	2	3	4	FINAL
Fresno State	3	14	0	3	20
Cincinnati	14	7	0	7	28

1st quarter
12:48 - CIN Guidugli 33 pass from Pike (Rogers kick)
7:47 - FRES Goessling 36 FG
5:48 - CIN Gilyard 11 pass from Pike (Rogers kick)

2nd quarter
11:48 - FRES Mathews 1 run (Goessling kick)
8:55 - CIN Pead 1 run (Rogers kick)
0:07 - FRES Hamler 21 pass from Colburn (Goessling kick)

4th quarter
13:09 - CIN Gilyard 23 pass from Pike (Rogers kick)
8:09 - FRES Goesling 49 FG

Fresno State stats
RUSHING LEADERS: Mathews 38-145-1, Miller 10-77-0, Rouse 5-50-0
PASSING: LEADERS: Colburn 16-27-153-1 1 TD
RECEIVING LEADERS: Hamler 4-57-1, Kinter 4-27-0
TACKLING LEADERS: Herron 7, Jacobs 6, Jefferson 5
INTERCEPTIONS: 0

Cincinnati stats
RUSHING LEADERS: Pead 4-27-1, Pike 4-25-0, Ramsey 4-14-0
PASSING LEADERS: Pike 18-26-300-0 3 TD
RECEIVING LEADERS: Gilyard 9-177-2, Woods 4-53-0
TACKLING LEADERS: Frey 11, Schaffer 9, D. Jones 9, Giordano 9,
Webster 8, Wolfe 8
INTERCEPTIONS: Carey 1

Records: Cincinnati 4-0, Fresno State 1-3

Game 5
No. 10 CINCINNATI 37, MIAMI (OHIO) 13

Saturday, Oct. 3
Attendance: 23,493

Yager Stadium
Oxford, Ohio

"Today was not our 'A' game. Not to take anything away from Miami because they

played very well today. We've just got more work to do."

- Head coach Brian Kelly

For the second straight week, the Cincinnati defense came up with a big play late in the game, this time to help the Bearcats win in the annual Battle for the Victory Bell. Miami, the Bearcats' long-time neighborhood rival, trailed by 10 points late in the third quarter and had the ball on Cincinnati's three yard-line facing third and goal when Cincinnati linebacker JK Schaffer intercepted quarterback Zac Dysert's pass in the end zone. Cincinnati's Jacob Ramsey rushed for 103 yards and three touchdowns. Tony Pike completed 23 of 42 passes for 270 yards, with two touchdowns and one interception. Dysert was sacked seven times, four by Cincinnati defensive end Alex Daniels. Miami managed only 30 rushing yards on 35 carries. The Bearcats, who had entered the AP Top 10 that week for the first time in school history, were the first Top 10 team ever to play at Miami.

Score by quarter	1	2	3	4	FINAL
Cincinnati	13	10	0	14	37
Miami	0	7	6	0	13

228

1st quarter

4:12 - CIN Ramsey 4 run (kick failed)
0:00 - CIN Binns 35 pass from Pike (Rogers kick)

2nd quarter

12:33 - CIN Ramsey 8 run (Rogers kick)
4:21 - MIA Merriweather 1 run (Cook kick)
2:48 - CIN Rogers 42 FG

3rd quarter

5:00 - MIA Bratton 19 pass from Dysert (kick failed)

4th quarter

11:35 - CIN Ramsey 2 run (Rogers kick)
8:12 - CIN Gilyard 23 pass from Pike (Rogers kick)

Cincinnati stats

RUSHING LEADERS: Ramsey 12-103-3, Pead 5-60-0
PASSING LEADERS: Pike 23-42-270-1 2 TD
RECEIVING LEADERS: Gilyard 6-75-1, Barnett 6-57-0, Binns 5-83-1
TACKLING LEADERS: Revels 13, Daniels 8, Schaffer 8, D. Jones 7
INTERCEPTIONS: Waugh 1

Miami stats

RUSHING LEADERS: Bratton 12-30-0
PASSING LEADERS: Dysert 33-47-286-2 1 TD
RECEIVING LEADERS: Bratton 11-90-1, A. Robinson 10-100-0,
Harris 5-31-0
TACKLING LEADERS: Kokal 13, Wedge 9, Gafford 7
INTERCEPTIONS: Gilmore 1

Records: Cincinnati 5-0, Miami 0-5

Game 6
No. 8 CINCINNATI 34, No. 21 SOUTH FLORIDA 17

Thursday, Oct. 15   Raymond James Stadium
Attendance: 63,976   Tampa, Florida

"I didn't even see Tony go down. They put me in for a play (before halftime). I didn't think it was going to last, but we came into the locker room and they said to be ready. I was just thinking 'go through my reads and take care of the ball.'"

- Quarterback Zach Collaros

Cincinnati quarterback Tony Pike left the game after he fell on his left (non-throwing) arm following a hit by USF's Aaron Harris during the Bearcats' final offensive drive of the first half. He returned for one series at the start of the third quarter, then left the game for good when he was crushed while throwing an incomplete pass on third down. He was replaced by Zach Collaros, who ran for 75 yards and a touchdown on Cincinnati's next possession to give the Bearcats a 24-10 lead. Collaros finished with 132 rushing yards and two touchdowns. He also passed for 72 yards to lead the Bearcats to their 12th straight regular-season victory. Aaron Webster intercepted a pass and returned it 83 yards to set up a three-yard touchdown pass from Pike to Armon Binns early in the second quarter.

Score by quarter	1	2	3	4	FINAL
Cincinnati	3	14	7	10	34
South Florida	7	3	7	0	17

1st quarter
9:57 - CIN Rogers 37 FG
6:14 - USF Hester 28 pass from Daniels (Schwartz kick)

2nd quarter
14:38 - CIN Binns 3 pass from Pike (Rogers kick)
4:31 - CIN Binns 8 pass from Pike (Rogers kick)
0:00 - USF Schwartz 50 FG

3rd quarter
8:34 - CIN Collaros 75 run (Rogers kick)
0:33 - USF Daniels 1 run (Schwartz kick)

4th quarter
13:14 - CIN Collaros 3 run (Rogers kick)
6:39 - CIN Rogers 29 FG

Cincinnati stats
RUSHING LEADERS: Collaros 10-132-2, Pead 12-55-0
PASSING LEADERS: Pike 12-25-140-0 2 TD, Collaros 4-7-72-1 0 TD
RECEIVING LEADERS: Gilyard 5-75-0, Binns 4-31-2, Pead 3-30-0
TACKLING LEADERS: Revels 9, Giordano 7, Battle 6
INTERCEPTIONS: Frey 1, Webster 1

Souht Florida stats
RUSHING LEADERS: Daniels 16-74-1, Plancher 7-37-0
PASSING LEADERS: Daniels 15-32-208-2 1 TD
RECEIVING LEADERS: Richardson 4-36-0, Hester 3-41-1, Bogan 2-50-0
TACKLING LEADERS: Murphy 8, Wilson 8, Allen 7, Selvie 6
INTERCEPTIONS: Allen 1

Records: Cincinnati 6-0, South Florida 5-1

Game 7
No. 5 CINCINNATI 41, LOUISVILLE 10

Saturday, Oct. 24
Attendance: 35,099

Nippert Stadium
Cincinnati, Ohio

"I was hoping Tony Pike would actually play. It makes them one-dimensional

and is a better matchup for us. I knew Collaros could run."

- Louisville head coach Steve Kragthorpe

Making his first career start at quarterback, Zach Collaros completed 15 of 17 passes for 253 yards with three touchdowns and no interceptions in the annual battle for the Keg of Nails. He also ran 11 times for 52 yards to lead Cincinnati to its seventh win without a loss. Mardy Gilyard caught a touchdown pass to give him 22 for his career, which tied a school record. Cincinnati jumped out to a 21-0 lead before Louisville got on the scoreboard late in the first half. UC's defense held Louisville to 14 total yards in the first quarter with no first downs and no pass completions. After Louisville kicked a 36-yard field goal on its first possession of the second half, Gilyard returned the kickoff 75 yards to the Louisville 14 to set up Jake Rogers for a 25-yard field goal, the first of 20 unanswered points the Bearcats scored. Isaiah Pead gained 88 yards on six carries and scored three touchdowns, one of which came on a 67-yard run.

Score by quarter	1	2	3	4	FINAL
Louisville	0	7	3	0	10
Cincinnati	14	7	17	3	41

1st quarter

10:10 - CIN Pead 1 run (Rogers kick)
5:21 - CIN Binns 24 pass from Collaros (Rogers kick)

2nd quarter

9:01 - CIN Pead 15 pass from Collaros (Rogers kick)
1:01 - LOU Chichester 4 pass from Froman (Payne kick)

3rd quarter

10:27 - LOU Payne 36 FG
8:38 - CIN Rogers 25 FG
6:18 - CIN Gilyard 31 pass from Collaros (Rogers kick)
4:36 - CIN Pead 67 run (Rogers kick)

4th quarter

12:45 - CIN Rogers 45 FG

Louisville stats

RUSHING LEADERS: Ashley 13-67-0, Anderson 12-56-0
PASSING LEADERS: Stein 6-9-98-0 0 TD, Froman 6-10-42-0 1 TD
RECEIVING LEADERS: Graham 3-35-0, Beaumont 3-29-0,
Chichester 2-20-0-1
TACKLING LEADERS: Mathews 7, Thompson 6
INTERCEPTIONS: 0

Cincinnati stats

RUSHING LEADERS: Pead 6-88-2, Collaros 11-52-0
PASSING LEADERS: Collaros 15-17-253-0 3 TD
RECEIVING LEADERS: Gilyard 4-82-1, Binns 3-75-1, Woods 3-54-0
TACKLING LEADERS: Revels 11, Stewart 10, Davis 7, Schaffer 7
INTERCEPTIONS: Stewart 1

Records: Cincinnati 7-0, Louisville 2-5

Game 8
No. 5 CINCINNATI 28, SYRACUSE 7

Saturday, Oct. 31   Carrier Dome
Attendance: 33,802   Syracuse, New York

"I was concerned all week that if we did not match the level of intensity that Syracuse plays

with this year we would be in trouble. This was the one as a coach that I was worried

about."

- Head coach Brian Kelly

Quarterback Zach Collaros improvised on several plays and made them work to lead Cincinnati to a 28-7 victory. Collaros completed 22 of 28 passes for 295 yards and four touchdowns, two to Armon Binns. The first Bearcat score came on an 81-yard pass from Collaros to Binns, who caught five passes for 138 yards. On third-and-11 from the Cincinnati 19-yard line, Collaros was flushed out of the pocket when he saw Binns alone a few yards downfield. He flipped the ball to Binns, who sprinted down the sideline for a touchdown. In the second quarter, Collaros was the holder on an apparent field goal try by Jake Rogers, but mishandled the snap from Mike Windt. He rolled out and found tight end Kazeem Alli in the end zone for 16-yard touchdown. The Bearcats led, 14-7, at halftime thanks to an interception by Drew Frey just before intermission after Syracuse had moved to the Cincinnati eight-yard line. They scored two second-half touchdowns while the Cincinnati defense was shutting down the Orange on a day when the Bearcats out-gained Syracuse 422 yards to 283.

Score by quarter	1	2	3	4	FINAL
Cincinnati	7	7	7	7	28
Syracuse	7	0	0	0	7

1st quarter
7:24 - CIN Binns 81 pass from Collaros (Rogers kick)
5:13 - SYR Catalina 9 pass from Paulus (Lichtenstein kick)

2nd quarter
14:11 - CIN Alli 16 pass from Collaros (Rogers kick)

3rd quarter
12:15 - CIN Binns 13 pass from Collaros (Rogers kick)

4th quarter
9:53 - CIN Robinson 4 pass from Collaros (Rogers kick)

Cincinnati stats
RUSHING LEADERS: Pead 16-77-0, Ramsey 7-27-0, Collaros 9-22-0
PASSING LEADERS: Collaros 22-28-295-0 4 TD
RECEIVING LEADERS: Gilyard 6-62-0, Binns 5-138-2, Woods 3-32-0,
Alli 2-23-1, Robinson 2-21-1
TACKLING: Schaffer 8, Revels 5, B. Jones 5
INTERCEPTIONS: Frey 1

Syracuse stats
RUSHING LEADERS: Carter 19-50-0, Bailey 7-34-0
PASSING LEADERS: Paulus 12-17-85-1 1 TD, Nassib 7-10-97-0 0 TD
RECEIVING LEADERS: Davis 5-51-0, Williams 4-34-0, Bailey 3-39-0
TACKLING LEADERS: Holmes 10, Suter 8, Smith 7
INTERCEPTIONS: 0

Records: Cincinnati 8-0, Syracuse 3-5

Game 9
No. 4 CINCINNATI 47, CONNECTICUT 45

Saturday, Nov. 7   Nippert Stadium
Attendance: 35,100   Cincinnati, Ohio

"It was an amazing feeling being out there, especially when our offense was

clicking like that. It was really just a lot of fun."

- Quarterback Zach Collaros

Connecticut stormed back from a 37-17 deficit midway through the third quarter to pull within two points on Jordan Todman's two-yard touchdown run with 5:03 remaining. The Huskies chose to go for two, but quarterback Zach Fraser was sacked by Cincinnati's Curtis Young. Cincinnati then scored on a 14-yard run by Isaiah Pead to give the Bearcats a nine-point lead with 1:52 to go in the game. The Huskies came back again to get within two on Frazer's nine-yard pass to Marcus Easley with 13 seconds left. Cincinnati's Charley Howard sealed the win for the Bearcats when he recovered the Huskies' onside kick with 12 seconds remaining. Cincinnati quarterback Zach Collaros passed for 480 yards, the second-highest total in school history. He also rushed for 75 yards and two touchdowns. Running back Jacob Ramsey gained 91 yards on 12 carries. The Bearcats gained a school-record 711 yards. Mardy Gilyard caught 12 passes for 172 yards. Jacob Rogers kicked four field goals and was five-for-five on extra points.

Score by quarter	1	2	3	4	FINAL
Connecticut	7	3	14	21	45
Cincinnati	10	20	7	10	47

1st quarter
12:03 - CIN Pead 1 run (Rogers kick)
7:27 - CONN Todman 6 run (Teggart kick)
4:57 - CIN Rogers 41 FG

2nd quarter
14:12 - CIN Collaros 4 run (Rogers kick)
9:47 - CONN Teggart 42 FG
4:49 - CIN Rogers 27 FG
1:48 - CIN Binns 41 pass from Collaros (Rogers kick)
0:00 - CIN Rogers 34 FG

3rd quarter
9:59 - CONN Todman 46 run (Teggart kick)
7:03 - CIN Collaros 28 run (Rogers kick)
2:08 - CONN McClain 87 punt return (Teggart kick)

4th quarter
14:51 - CIN Rogers 35 FG
13:21 - CONN Todman 1 run (Easley pass from Todman)
5:03 - CONN Todman 2 run (pass failed)
1:52 - CIN Pead 14 run (Rogers kick)
0:13 - CONN Easley 9 pass from Frazer (Teggart kick)

Connecticut stats
RUSHING LEADERS: Todman 26-162-4, Dixon 8-27-0
PASSING LEADERS: Frazer 19-32-261-0 1 TD
RECEIVING LEADERS: Easley 6-87-1, Moore 4-77-0, Kanuch 3-36-0
TACKLING LEADERS: Wilson 11, Lutrus 9, Wreh-Wilson 9, McClain 8
INTERCEPTIONS: 0

Cincinnati stats
RUSHING LEADERS: Ramsey 12-91-0, Collaros 13-75-2, Pead 10-67-2
PASSING LEADERS: Collaros 29-37-480-0 1 TD
RECEIVING LEADERS: Gilyard 12-172-0, Binns 5-108-1, Woods 5-68-0, Ramsey 3-18-0, Robinson 2-74-0
TACKLING LEADERS: Battle 10, Revels 10, Schaffer 8
INTERCEPTIONS: 0

Records: Cincinnati 9-0, Connecticut 4-5

Game 10
No. 5 CINCINNATI 24, No. 23 WEST VIRGINIA 21

Friday, Nov. 13
Attendance: 35,105

Nippert Stadium
Cincinnati, Ohio

"When we got to the red zone, (Kelly) said, 'Pike!' I thought he was

calling me to talk about a play or something. He told me to go in.

I kind of had some trouble getting my chin strap buttoned."

- Quarterback Tony Pike

The Bearcats became the first team in school history to start a season with a 10-0 record behind Isaiah Pead, who carried 18 times for a career-high 175 yards with one touchdown. Tony Pike made his first appearance at quarterback since he was injured on Oct. 15 at South Florida. He entered the game in the first quarter when Cincinnati reached the red zone and promptly threw a 10-yard touchdown pass to Armon Binns. With the score tied at 14-14, Pike entered the game again on the Bearcats' first possession of the second half and threw another touchdown pass, this time to D.J. Woods for six yards to give Cincinnati a 21-14 lead. The Bearcats increased their lead to 24-14 on Jake Rogers' 38-yard field goal with 2:08 remaining. Cincinnati had its first lost fumble of the season when Adrien Robinson coughed up the ball at the Cincinnati 49-yard line after catching a Zach Collaros pass. Collaros completed 17 of 24 passes for 205 yards with one interception. He also ran for 44 yards on 10 carries.

Score by quarter	1	2	3	4	FINAL
West Virginia	7	7	0	7	21
Cincinnati	7	7	7	3	24

238

1st quarter

9:56 - CIN Binns 10 pass from Pike (Rogers kick)
3:19 - WVU Brown 8 run (Bitancurt kick)

2nd quarter

8:05 - WVU Clarke 37 run (Bitancurt kick)
5:26 - CIN Pead 2 run (Rogers kick)

3rd quarter

11:07 - CIN Woods 6 pass from Pike (Rogers kick)

4th quarter

2:08 - CIN Rogers 38 FG
0:39 - WVU Starks 3 pass from Brown (Bitancurt kick)

West Virginia stats

RUSHING LEADERS: Devine 25-88-0, Clarke 5-60-1
PASSING LEADERS: Brown 17-25-188-0 1 TD
RECEIVING LEADERS: Starks 5-50-1, Sanders 4-42-0,
TACKLING LEADERS: Hogan 11, Thomas 7, Lazear 6
INTERCEPTIONS: Sands 1

Cincinnati stats

RUSHING LEADERS: Pead 18-175-1, Collaros 10-44-0
PASSING LEADERS: Collaros 17-24-205-1 0 TD, Pike 2-4-16-0 2 TD
RECEIVING LEADERS: Binns 5-62-1, Robinson 3-59-0, Woods 3-40-1,
Gilyard 3-22-0
TACKLING LEADERS: Revels 13, Schaffer 8, Stewart 7
INTERCEPTIONS: 0

Records: Cincinnati 10-0, West Virginia 7-3

Game 11
No. 5 CINCINNATI 49, ILLINOIS 36

Friday, Nov. 27   Nippert Stadium
Attendance: 35,106   Cincinnati, Ohio

"He was here. I think he knew Pike broke his record, but he was

happy because I was part of it. He's living through this Bearcats

team just like anybody else. He's loving it more than anybody else."

- Tight end Ben Guidugli, referring to his brother Gino

In his final game at Nippert Stadium, Tony Pike returned to the starting lineup and celebrated by passing for 399 yards and setting a school record for touchdown passes in a game with six, breaking the previous record of five held by Gino Guidugli in 2004. The Bearcats built a 28-7 lead early in the second quarter, led 35-20 at halftime and 42-20 after Pike's ten-yard touchdown pass to Armon Binns with 4:43 left in the third quarter. Illinois came back to get within 12 points, but Cincinnati sealed the win with a 21-yard touchdown pass from Pike to Mardy Gilyard with 4:19 left. Gilyard caught the 23rd and 24th touchdown passes of his career to break Dominick Goodman's school record. He also set a school record with his third career kickoff return for a touchdown that enabled the Bearcats to erase an early 7-0 deficit. Tight end Ben Guidugli caught seven passes for a career-high 149 yards and two touchdowns, helping Pike break his brother's record.

Score by quarter	1	2	3	4	FINAL
Illinois	7	13	3	13	36
Cincinnati	21	14	7	7	49

1st quarter
7:38 - ILL Sykes 21 pass from Williams (Dimke kick)
7:25 - CIN Gilyard 90 kickoff return (Rogers kick)
5:56 - CIN Guidugli 59 pass from Pike (Rogers kick)
1:50 - CIN Woods 6 pass from Pike (Rogers kick)

2nd quarter
14:28 - CIN Guidugli 2 pass from Pike (Rogers kick)
11:21 - ILL Duvalt 19 pass from Williams (Dimke kick)
6:01 - ILL Dimke 39 FG
4:04 - CIN Gilyard 11 pass from Pike (Rogers kick)
0:00 - ILL Dimke 48 FG

3rd quarter
4:43 - CIN Binns 10 pass from Pike (Rogers kick)
1:38 - ILL Dimke 30 FG

4th quarter
10:03 - ILL Williams 2 run (Dimke kick)
4:19 - CIN Gilyard 21 pass from Pike (Rogers kick)
2:54 - ILL – Sykes 7 pass from Williams (pass intercepted)

Illinois stats
RUSHING LEADERS: Williams 11-67-1
PASSING LEADERS: Williams 21-34-282-0 3 TD
RECEIVING LEADERS: Duvalt 6-94-1, Benn 3-59-0, Sykes 3-32-2,
Leshoure 3-17-0
TACKLING LEADERS: Edwards 7, Thomas 6, Wilson 5, Bussey 5
INTERCEPTIONS: 0

Cincinnati stats
RUSHING LEADERS: Goebel 5-23-0, Collaros 2-12-0
PASSING LEADERS: Pike 32-46-399-0 6 TD
RECEIVING LEADERS: Guidugli 7-149-2, Gilyard 7-102-2, Binns 7-62-1,
Woods 7-53-1
TACKLING LEADERS: Schaffer 14, Young 8, Revels 7
INTERCEPTIONS: 0

Records: Cincinnati 11-0, Illinois 3-8

Game 12
No. 5 CINCINNATI 45, No. 14 PITTSBURGH 44

Saturday, Dec. 5   Heinz Field
Attendance: 63,387   Pittsburgh, Pennsylvania

"I told our players I was honored to be their head football coach because

we're not perfect, and we know we're not perfect, and we don't apologize

for not being perfect. We just keep fighting and that's out spirit. That's who we are."

- Head coach Brian Kelly

Trailing 31-10 in the first half, Cincinnati received a spark when Mardy Gilyard returned a kickoff 99 yards for a touchdown with 1:10 left in the half. The Bearcats came back to tie the score on Isaiah Pead's one-yard touchdown run with 5:46 left. Pitt broke the tie on Dion Lewis' five-yead touchdown run with 1:36 to play, but a botched hold prevented the Panthers from kicking the extra point. The Bearcats then drove down the field, covering 61 yards in four plays. Tony Pike's 29-yard touchdown pass to Armon Binns tied the score at 44-44 with 33 seconds left and Jake Rogers' extra point kick gave Cincinnati a one-point lead that stood up over the final 33 seconds, making Cincinnati the Big East champion for the second straight season. Pike overcome a sub-standard first half to complete 22 of 44 passes for 302 yards and three touchdowns with three interceptions. Gilyard caught five passes for 118 yards and a 68-yard touchdown reception. Pitt's Lewis rushed for 194 yards on 47 carries with three touchdowns.

Score by quarter	1	2	3	4	FINAL
Cincinnati	7	10	7	21	45
Pittsburgh	7	24	0	13	44

1st quarter

7:27 - PITT Lewis 4 run (Hutchins kick)
5:17 - CIN Ramsey 2 run (Rogers kick)

2nd quarter

14:13 - PITT Baldwin 22 pass from Stull (Hutchins kick)
11:12 - CIN Rogers 20 FG
10:28 - PITT Baldwin 40 pass from Stull (Hutchins kick)
4:53 - PITT Hutchins 33 FG
1:26 - PITT Stull 3 run (Hutchins kick)
1:10 - CIN Gilyard 99 kickoff return (Rogers kick)

3rd quarter

8:12 - CIN Gilyard 68 pass from Pike (Rogers kick)

4th quarter

12:26 - PITT Lewis 15 run (Hutchins kick)
11:09 - CIN Woods 8 pass from Pike (kick failed)
5:46 - CIN Pead 1 run (Gilyard pass from Pike)
1:36 - PITT Lewis 5 run (run failed)
0:33 - CIN Binns 29 pass from Pike (Rogers kick)

Cincinnati stats

RUSHING LEADERS: Pead 9-76-1
PASSING LEADERS: Pike 22-44- 302-3 3 TD
RECEIVING LEADERS: Woods 7-61-1, Gilyard 5-118-1 Binns 5-104-1,
Guidugli 3-17-0
TACKLING LEADERS: Webster 9, Schaffer 9, Young 8, Revels 7, Frey 7
INTERCEPTIONS: Webster 1, Battle 1

Pittsburgh stats

RUSHING LEADERS: Lewis 47-194-3
PASSING LEADERS: Stull 13-21-176-2 2 TD
RECEIVING LEADERS: Baldwin 6-113-2, Lewis 5-34-0
TACKLING LEADERS: Chappel 7, Holley 5, Gunn 5
INTERCEPTIONS: Holley 1, Fields 1, DeCicco 1

Records: Cincinnati 12-0, Pittsburgh 9-3

Sugar Bowl
No. 5 FLORIDA 51, No. 4 CINCINNATI 24

Friday, Jan. 1
Attendance: 65,207

Louisiana Superdome
New Orleans, Louisiana

"Obviously, coming into the football game being 12-0, the outcome of tonight's contest certainly wasn't the way we expected it to go. I couldn't be more proud of our young men battling the way they did all year."

- Interim head coach Jeff Quinn

Playing his final collegiate game, Florida quarterback Tim Tebow completed a career-high 31 passes in 35 attempts for a Sugar Bowl 482 yards – also a career high – and three touchdowns. He also rushed for 51 yards giving him a total of 533 yards, a record for a BCS bowl game. Tebow did not throw an incomplete pass until the 12:32 mark of the second quarter after he had completed a Sugar Bowl record 12 straight passes. Florida scored on five of its first six possessions – four touchdowns and a field goal. Cincinnati's usually prolific offense managed only 55 yards in the first half and 246 overall compared with a record BCS record-tying 659 yards for Florida. The Gators led, 37-3, early in the second half before the Bearcats made the score more respectable with 21 second-half points. Cincinnati was coached by interim head coach Jeff Quinn, the offensive coordinator who filled in for Brian Kelly after Kelly left to become the head coach at Notre Dame. Quarterback Tony Pike was 27-for-45 for 170 yards and three touchdowns in his final game at Cincinnati.

Score by quarter	1	2	3	4	FINAL
Florida	9	21	14	7	51
Cincinnati	0	3	7	14	24

1st quarter

6:13 - FLA Hernandez 7 pass from Tebow (kick failed)
1:20 - FLA Sturgis 40 FG

2nd quarter

9:07 - FLA Thompson 7 pass from Tebow (Sturgis kick)
7:05 - FLA Moody 6 run (Sturgis kick)
3:11 - CIN Rogers 47 FG
3:02 - FLA Cooper 80 pass from Tebow (Sturgis kick)

3rd quarter

11:13 - FLA Moody 2 run (Sturgis kick)
4:46 - CIN Waugh 2 pass from Pike (Rogers kick)
2:06 - FLA Tebow 4 run (Sturgis kick)

4th quarter

10:07 - CIN Binns 3 pass from Pike (Rogers kick)
7:06 - FLA Rainey 6 run (Sturgis kick)
3:43 - CIN Alli 6 pass from Pike (Rogers kick)

Cincinnati stats

RUSHING LEADERS: Pead 7-48-0
PASSING LEADERS: Pike 27-45-170-0 3 TD
RECEIVING LEADERS: Gilyard 7-41-0, Binns 5-29-1, Guidugli 5-22-0
TACKLING LEADERS: Schaffer 10, Battle 8, Webster 7, Stewart 7
INTERCEPTIONS: 0

Florida stats

RUSHING LEADERS: Gillislee 5-78-0, Tebow 14-51-1
PASSING LEADERS: Tebow 31-35-482-0 3 TD
RECEIVING LEADERS: Hernandez 9-111-1, Cooper 7-181-1,
Thompson 5-63-0
TACKLING LEADERS: Spikes 6, Haden 6, Hicks 6
INTERCEPTIONS: 0

Records: Cincinnati 12-1, Florida 13-1

Source: Sports-reference.com

2009 Cincinnati Overall Team Statistics

TEAM STATISTICS	CIN	OPP
SCORING	502	300
Points Per Game	38.6	23.1
Points Off Turnovers	52	20
FIRST DOWNS	270	267
Rushing	89	106
Passing	164	147
Penalty	17	14
RUSHING YARDAGE	1803	1869
Yards gained rushing	2057	2266
Yards lost rushing	254	397
Rushing Attempts	361	515
Average Per Rush	5.0	3.6
Average Per Game	138.7	143.8
TDs Rushing	23	20
PASSING YARDAGE	4014	2993
Comp-Att-Int	311-472-8	267-420-16
Average Per Pass	8.5	7.1
Average Per Catch	12.9	11.2
Average Per Game	308.8	230.2
TDs Passing	39	16
TOTAL OFFENSE	5817	4862
Total Plays	833	935
Average Per Play	7.0	5.2
Average Per Game	447.5	374.0
KICK RETURNS: #-Yards	54-1540	69-1410
PUNT RETURNS: #-Yards	19-247	24-264
INT RETURNS: #-Yards	16-189	8-102
KICK RETURN AVERAGE	28.5	20.4
PUNT RETURN AVERAGE	13.0	11.0
INT RETURN AVERAGE	11.8	12.8
FUMBLES-LOST	11-2	12-3
PENALTIES-Yards	63-589	82-672
Average Per Game	45.3	51.7
PUNTS-Yards	52-2074	75-3161
Average Per Punt	39.9	42.1
Net punt average	33.7	37.5
KICKOFFS-Yards	92-6158	60-3775
Average Per Kick	66.9	62.9
Net kick average	46.6	35.6
TIME OF POSSESSION/Game	25:48	34:02

| 3RD-DOWN Conversions | 58/142 | 81/205 |
| 3rd-Down Pct | 41% | 40% |

TEAM STATISTICS	CIN	OPP
4TH-DOWN Conversions	9/13	18/27
4th-Down Pct	69%	67%
SACKS BY-Yards	37-244	15-96
MISC YARDS	0	0
TOUCHDOWNS SCORED	66	37
FIELD GOALS-ATTEMPTS	13-19	14-16
ON-SIDE KICKS	0-0	1-3
RED-ZONE SCORES	(51-58) 88%	(37-42) 88%
RED-ZONE TOUCHDOWNS	(42-58) 72%	(30-42) 71%
PAT-ATTEMPTS	(63-65) 97%	(30-32) 94%
ATTENDANCE	203,741	280,304
Games/Avg Per Game	6/33,957	6/46,717
Neutral Site Games	1/65,207	

SCORE BY QUARTERS	1st	2nd	3rd	4th	Total
Cincinnati	124	172	94	112	502
Opponents	70	101	54	75	300

2009 Cincinnati Overall Individual Statistics

RUSHING	GP	Att	Gain	Loss	Net	Avg	TD	Long	Avg/G
PEAD, I.	13	121	843	37	806	6.7	9	67	62.0
RAMSEY, J.	12	74	471	32	439	5.9	4	62	36.6
COLLAROS	12	57	371	27	344	6.0	4	75	28.7
KELCE, T.	11	8	47	0	47	5.9	2	19	4.3
GOEBEL, J.	9	12	47	6	41	3.4	0	8	4.6
WILLIAMS, D.	13	17	48	11	37	2.2	0	10	2.8
JOHNSON, S.	7	2	35	0	35	17.5	1	33	5.0
ANDERSON	4	8	35	8	27	3.4	0	10	6.8
KAY, B.	2	4	24	0	24	6.0	0	8	12.0
GILYARD, M.	13	5	16	0	16	3.2	1	5	1.2
WINN, G.	1	5	16	4	12	2.4	0	6	12.0
PIKE, T.	10	31	95	89	6	0.2	2	16	0.6
HINES, Q.	3	2	6	1	5	2.5	0	6	1.7
ROGERS, J.	13	1	3	0	3	3.0	0	3	0.2
TEAM	11	14	0	39	-39	-2.8	0	0	-3.5
Total..........	13	361	2057	254	1803	5.0	23	75	138.7
Opponents......13		515	2266	397	1869	3.6	20	52	143.8

PASSING	G	Effic	Cmp-Att-Int	Pct	Yds	TD	Lng	Avg/G
PIKE, T.	10	149.82	211-338-6	62.4	2520	29	68	252.0
COLLAROS	12	195.53	93-124-2	75.0	1434	10	81	119.5
ANDERSON	4	129.53	5-6-0	83.3	33	0	13	8.2
KAY, B.	2	213.40	2-2-0	100.0	27	0	19	13.5
TEAM	11	0.00	0-2-0	0.0	0	0	0	0.0
Total..........	13	161.20	311-472-8	65.9	4014	39	81	308.8
Opponents......13		128.38	267-420-16	63.6	2993	16	80	230.2

RECEIVING	G	No.	Yds	Avg	TD	Long	Avg/G
GILYARD, M.	13	87	1191	13.7	11	68	91.6
BINNS, A.	13	61	888	14.6	11	81	68.3
WOODS, DJ	12	51	640	12.5	4	45	53.3
GUIDUGLI, B.	13	27	364	13.5	3	59	28.0
PEAD, I.	13	20	201	10.1	2	41	15.5
RAMSEY, J.	12	18	145	8.1	2	32	12.1
ALLI, K.	13	12	156	13.0	2	38	12.0
ROBINSON, A.	10	10	174	17.4	1	54	17.4
BARNETT, M.	9	10	95	9.5	1	21	10.6
WILLIAMS, D.	13	4	14	3.5	0	5	1.1
HOWARD, J.	5	3	50	16.7	0	32	10.0
HOWARD, C.	13	2	52	26.0	1	43	4.0
GOEBEL, J.	9	2	12	6.0	0	9	1.3
WINN, G.	1	1	19	19.0	0	19	19.0
PAYNE, L.	3	1	8	8.0	0	8	2.7
KELCE, T.	11	1	3	3.0	0	3	0.3
WAUGH, M.	13	1	2	2.0	1	2	0.2
Total..........	13	311	4014	12.9	39	81	308.8
Opponents......	13	267	2993	11.2	16	80	230.2

PUNT RETURNS	No.	Yds	Avg	TD	Long
GILYARD, M.	16	202	12.6	1	53
WOODS, DJ	3	45	15.0	0	27
Total..........	19	247	13.0	1	53
Opponents......	24	264	11.0	1	87

INTERCEPTIONS	No.	Yds	Avg	TD	Long
WEBSTER, A.	4	135	33.8	0	83
SCHAFFER, JK	3	23	7.7	0	13
FREY, D.	2	0	0.0	0	0
BATTLE, D.	2	0	0.0	0	0
JONES, D.	1	-2	-2.0	0	0
REVELS, A.	1	0	0.0	0	0
CAREY, C.	1	21	21.0	0	21
STEWART, W.	1	-2	-2.0	0	0
WAUGH, M.	1	14	14.0	0	14
Total..........	16	189	11.8	0	83

This is What the Top Feels Like

Opponents......	8	102	12.8	0	30

KICK RETURNS	No.	Yds	Avg	TD	Long
GILYARD, M.	42	1281	30.5	2	99
WILLIAMS, D.	8	245	30.6	1	100
THOMPSON, R.	2	0	0.0	0	0
HOWARD, C.	1	0	0.0	0	0
BARNETT, M.	1	14	14.0	0	14
Total.........	54	1540	28.5	3	100
Opponents......	69	1410	20.4	0	51

FUMBLE RETURNS	No.	Yds	Avg	TD	Long
JOHNSON, R.	1	4	4.0	0	4
Total.........	1	4	4.0	0	4
Opponents......	0	0	0.0	0	0

SCORING	TD	FGs	Kick	Rcv	Pass	Saf	Points
ROGERS, J.	0	13-19	63-65	0	0-0	0	102
GILYARD, M.	15	0-0	0-0	1	0-0	0	92
BINNS, A.	11	0-0	0-0	0	0-0	0	66
PEAD, I.	11	0-0	0-0	0	0-0	0	66
RAMSEY, J.	6	0-0	0-0	0	0-0	0	36
COLLAROS, Z.	4	0-0	0-0	0	0-0	0	24
WOODS, DJ	4	0-0	0-0	0	0-0	0	24
GUIDUGLI, B.	3	0-0	0-0	0	0-0	0	18
KELCE, T.	2	0-0	0-0	0	0-0	0	12
ALLI, K.	2	0-0	0-0	0	0-0	0	12
PIKE, T.	2	0-0	0-0	0	1-1	0	12
WAUGH, M.	1	0-0	0-0	0	0-0	0	6
ROBINSON, A.	1	0-0	0-0	0	0-0	0	6
WILLIAMS, D.	1	0-0	0-0	0	0-0	0	6
JOHNSON, S.	1	0-0	0-0	0	0-0	0	6
HOWARD, C.	1	0-0	0-0	0	0-0	0	6
BARNETT, M.	1	0-0	0-0	0	0-0	0	6
TEAM	0	0-0	0-0	0	0-0	1	2
Total.........	66	13-19	63-65	1	1-1	1	502
Opponents......	37	14-16	30-32	2	2-4	1	300

TOTAL OFFENSE	G	Plays	Rush	Pass	Total	Avg/G
PIKE, T.	10	369	6	2520	2526	252.6
COLLAROS, Z.	12	181	344	1434	1778	148.2
PEAD, I.	13	121	806	0	806	62.0
RAMSEY, J.	12	74	439	0	439	36.6
ANDERSON, C.	4	14	27	33	60	15.0
KAY, B.	2	6	24	27	51	25.5
KELCE, T.	11	8	47	0	47	4.3
GOEBEL, J.	9	12	41	0	41	4.6
WILLIAMS, D.	13	17	37	0	37	2.8
JOHNSON, S.	7	2	35	0	35	5.0
GILYARD, M.	13	5	16	0	16	1.2
WINN, G.	1	5	12	0	12	12.0
HINES, Q.	3	2	5	0	5	1.7
ROGERS, J.	13	1	3	0	3	0.2
TEAM	11	16	-39	0	-39	-3.5
Total..........	13	833	1803	4014	5817	447.5
Opponents......	13	935	1869	2993	4862	374.0

FIELD GOALS	FGM-FGA	Pct	01-19	20-29	30-39	40-49	50-99	Lg	B
ROGERS, J.	13-19	68.4	0-0	4-4	5-7	4-6	0-2	47	0

PUNTING	No.	Yds	Avg	Long	TB	FC	I20	50+	Blkd
ROGERS, J.	43	1788	41.6	54	3	8	15	8	1
O'DONNELL, P.	7	265	37.9	50	0	0	2	1	0
TEAM	1	0	0.0	0	0	0	0	0	0
PIKE, T.	1	21	21.0	21	0	0	0	0	0
Total..........	52	2074	39.9	54	3	8	17	9	1
Opponents......	75	3161	42.1	62	5	26	18	16	0

KICKOFFS	No.	Yds	Avg	TB	OB	Retn	Net	YdLn
ROGERS, J.	92	6158	66.9	23	0			
Total..........	92	6158	66.9	23	0	1410	46.6	23
Opponents......	60	3775	62.9	5	1	1540	35.6	34

ALL PURPOSE	G	Rush	Rec	PR	KOR	IR	Tot	Avg/G
GILYARD, M.	13	16	1191	202	1281	0	2690	206.9
PEAD, I.	13	806	201	0	0	0	1007	77.5
BINNS, A.	13	0	888	0	0	0	888	68.3
WOODS, DJ	12	0	640	45	0	0	685	57.1
RAMSEY, J.	12	439	145	0	0	0	584	48.7
GUIDUGLI, B.	13	0	364	0	0	0	364	28.0
COLLAROS, Z.	12	344	0	0	0	0	344	28.7
WILLIAMS, D.	13	37	14	0	245	0	296	22.8
ROBINSON, A.	10	0	174	0	0	0	174	17.4
ALLI, K.	13	0	156	0	0	0	156	12.0
WEBSTER, A.	13	0	0	0	0	135	135	10.4
BARNETT, M.	9	0	95	0	14	0	109	12.1
GOEBEL, J.	9	41	12	0	0	0	53	5.9
HOWARD, C.	13	0	52	0	0	0	52	4.0
KELCE, T.	11	47	3	0	0	0	50	4.5
HOWARD, J.	5	0	50	0	0	0	50	10.0
JOHNSON, S.	7	35	0	0	0	0	35	5.0
WINN, G.	1	12	19	0	0	0	31	31.0
ANDERSON, C.	4	27	0	0	0	0	27	6.8
KAY, B.	2	24	0	0	0	0	24	12.0
SCHAFFER, JK	13	0	0	0	0	23	23	1.8
CAREY, C.	13	0	0	0	0	21	21	1.6
WAUGH, M.	13	0	2	0	0	14	16	1.2
PAYNE, L.	3	0	8	0	0	0	8	2.7
PIKE, T.	10	6	0	0	0	0	6	0.6
HINES, Q.	3	5	0	0	0	0	5	1.7
ROGERS, J.	13	3	0	0	0	0	3	0.2
STEWART, W.	13	0	0	0	0	-2	-2	-0.2
JONES, D.	10	0	0	0	0	-2	-2	-0.2
TEAM	11	-39	0	0	0	0	-39	-3.5
Total..........	13	1803	4014	247	1540	189	7793	599.5
Opponents......	13	1869	2993	264	1410	102	6638	510.6

Source: University of Cincinnati

2009 Cincinnati Overall Defensive Statistics

	DEFENSIVE LEADERS	GP-GS	Solo	Ast	Total	TFL/Yds	No-Yards	Int-Yds	BrUp	QBH	Rcv-Yds	FF	Kick	Saf
50	REVELS, A.	13-13	45	64	109	4.5-6		1-0	2					
37	SCHAFFER, JK	13-12	54	46	100	5.5-21	1.5-11	3-23	3					
17	WEBSTER, A.	13-13	41	28	69	2.0-3		4-135	5			2		
26	FREY, D.	12-12	39	25	64	3.5-18	1.0-6	2-0	4	1				
9	BATTLE, D.	12-12	44	16	60	4.0-10		2-0	4	1		1		
54	STEWART, W.	13-11	33	26	59	8.5-39	4.5-32	1--2		1		1		
4	DANIELS, A.	13-12	22	34	56	11.0-66	8.5-61		1	3				
25	JONES, B.	13-13	40	12	52	3.5-10			1					
98	YOUNG, C.	10-10	31	19	50	11.0-30	2.0-12			5				
90	MATHEWS, R.	13-13	19	25	44	12.5-50	3.5-26			2				
99	GIORDANO, D.	13-0	13	29	42	7.0-20	2.0-5		1	4				
95	WOLFE, D.	13-13	21	20	41	8.0-38	5.0-32			1	1-0	1		
2D	JONES, D.	10-4	21	15	36	5.0-10		1--2				1		
42	DAVIS, D.	13-0	14	12	26	1.0-1			1					
58	MILLS, B.	13-0	15	10	25	8.0-33	3.5-28			1				
40	HUGHES, J.	13-1	9	14	23	6.0-15	2.0-5			1		1		
24	RICHARDSON, W.	13-0	13	8	21	0.5-1								
87	HOWARD, C.	13-0	9	9	18									
43	ARMSTRONG, R.	4-0	8	7	15	1.0-12	1.0-12	1-21						
7D	CAREY, C.	13-1	3	12	15	2.5-9	1.5-7			1		1		
21	CHEATHAM, C.	13-1	5	8	13			1-14						
35	WAUGH, M.	13-1	5	6	11	0.5-1								
81	HILTON, T.	13-0	7	4	11									
11	MCCAFFERTY, C.	13-0	4	4	8							1		
13	LAMBERT, P.	13-0	3	4	7									
84	WOODARD, O.	13-0	5	2	7						1-0			
48	BOMAR, M.	9-0	5	2	7									
45	TRIGG, R.	2-0	3	3	6	2.5-10								
97	ROGERS, J.	13-0	5		5					1				
5	JOHNSON, R.	11-0	4	1	5									
22	GOEBEL, J.	9-0	2	2	4						1-4			
55	COOK, A.	2-0	1	2	3									

About the Author

Bill Koch is a Cincinnati native and UC graduate. During his career as a Cincinnati sports writer, he has primarily covered UC athletics, but has also been the featured columnist at The Cincinnati Post. He has covered preps, was the beat writer for Xavier basketball for three years, and has written extensively about the Reds and Major League Baseball. Koch is the author of six previous books: The Pride of Price Hill, Nothing Changes, I Can't Believe I Got Paid for This, Inside the Crosstown Shootout, Best of the Bearcats and The Forgotten Bearcats.

Made in the USA
Columbia, SC
16 October 2020